The PR Campaigns
Worktext

Sara Miller McCune founded SAGE Publishing in 1965 to support the dissemination of usable knowledge and educate a global community. SAGE publishes more than 1000 journals and over 800 new books each year, spanning a wide range of subject areas. Our growing selection of library products includes archives, data, case studies and video. SAGE remains majority owned by our founder and after her lifetime will become owned by a charitable trust that secures the company's continued independence.

Los Angeles | London | New Delhi | Singapore | Washington DC | Melbourne

The PR Campaigns Worktext

Maria Elles Scott

Emerson College

Los Angeles | London | New Delhi
Singapore | Washington DC | Melbourne

FOR INFORMATION:

SAGE Publications, Inc.
2455 Teller Road
Thousand Oaks, California 91320
E-mail: order@sagepub.com

SAGE Publications Ltd.
1 Oliver's Yard
55 City Road
London, EC1Y 1SP
United Kingdom

SAGE Publications India Pvt. Ltd.
B 1/I 1 Mohan Cooperative Industrial Area
Mathura Road, New Delhi 110 044
India

SAGE Publications Asia-Pacific Pte. Ltd.
18 Cross Street #10-10/11/12
China Square Central
Singapore 048423

Printed in the United States of America

ISBN: 978-1-5443-9757-3

Acquisitions Editor: Lily Norton
Editorial Assistant: Sarah Wilson
Production Editor: Megha Negi
Copy Editor: Deanna Noga
Typesetter: Hurix Digital
Proofreader: Lawrence W. Baker
Indexer: Integra
Cover Designer: Dally Verghese
Marketing Manager: Staci Wittek

This book is printed on acid-free paper.

20 21 22 23 24 10 9 8 7 6 5 4 3 2 1

BRIEF CONTENTS

DETAILED CONTENTS

PR CAMPAIGNS CHECKLIST

THE PLAN OUTLINE

ITEMS TO CREATE	Draft Date	Completed	Final Date	Completed
Cover Page	_____	☐	_____	☐
Executive Summary	_____	☐	_____	☐
Table of Contents	_____	☐	_____	☐
Issue Statement	_____	☐	_____	☐
Goal (Typically One Sentence)	_____	☐	_____	☐
Situation Analysis	_____	☐	_____	☐
SWOT	_____	☐	_____	☐
Primary Focus (Target Audience)	_____	☐	_____	☐
Demographics	_____	☐	_____	☐
Psychographics	_____	☐	_____	☐
Prepackaged Audiences and Opinion Leaders	_____	☐	_____	☐
Research	_____	☐	_____	☐
Executive Summary	_____	☐	_____	☐
Secondary Research Summary	_____	☐	_____	☐
Reference List	_____	☐	_____	☐
Primary Research Introduction	_____	☐	_____	☐

Pitch	_____	▢	_____	▢
Release	_____	▢	_____	▢
Design Samples	_____	▢	_____	▢
Banners/Posters	_____	▢	_____	▢
E-vites	_____	▢	_____	▢
Flyers	_____	▢	_____	▢
PowerPoint	_____	▢	_____	▢
Promotional Samples	_____	▢	_____	▢
Video Samples/Stills	_____	▢	_____	▢
Primary Research	_____	▢	_____	▢
Interview/Survey Questions	_____	▢	_____	▢
Interview/Survey Results	_____	▢	_____	▢
(SPSS and Excel)	_____	▢	_____	▢
Research Correlations	_____	▢	_____	▢
Secondary Research	_____	▢	_____	▢
Reference List (A–Z, APA Format)	_____	▢	_____	▢
Original Articles	_____	▢	_____	▢
PowerPoint for Client	_____	▢	_____	▢

THE PRESENTATION OUTLINE

NOTE: The final presentation is 20 to 25 minutes with 10 minutes for questions and 10 minutes for a tour of physical work and project created. All speakers must audition for the role. The entire presentation is memorized; no notecards are used.

ITEMS TO CREATE	Draft Date	Completed	Final Date	Completed
Welcome Slide	_____	☐	_____	☐
Challenge/Issue Statement	_____	☐	_____	☐
Explanation of Focuses	_____	☐	_____	☐
Situation Analysis and SWOT	_____	☐	_____	☐
Start with those that cross-over and then move to ones that vary by focus	_____	☐	_____	☐
Primary Focus (by TEAM)	_____	☐	_____	☐
Define basic TA for entire program, and then split per focus	_____	☐	_____	☐
Research Introduction	_____	☐	_____	☐
Second Research	_____	☐	_____	☐
Key Points of What We Learned	_____	☐	_____	☐
Primary Research	_____	☐	_____	☐
Methods	_____	☐	_____	☐
Demographics	_____	☐	_____	☐
Research Summary	_____	☐	_____	☐
Results of Primary and Secondary Research	_____	☐	_____	☐
Goal Statement	_____	☐	_____	☐
Objectives	_____	☐	_____	☐
Messages and Themes, Style Guide	_____	☐	_____	☐
Strategies and Tactics	_____	☐	_____	☐

Strategies _____   _____   ☐   _____   ☐

Strategies _____   _____   ☐   _____   ☐

Strategies _____   _____   ☐   _____   ☐

Strategies _____   _____   ☐   _____   ☐

Evaluations (Usually Organized by Objective)   _____   ☐   _____   ☐

    Methods   _____   ☐   _____   ☐

Recommendations   _____   ☐   _____   ☐

Questions   _____   ☐   _____   ☐

PREFACE

WHY PUBLIC RELATIONS?

After more than a decade of teaching Public Relations (PR) and more than 20 years working in communications either as a journalist or a PR practitioner, I always fall back to "Why Public Relations?"

My answer is usually simple. I loved the storytelling aspect of journalism. I found the challenge of selecting just the right word to bring someone to tears or move someone to be a gift. I felt that it was an honor to be the voice of a group and to share their story with the masses. You must do so within the ethical confines of your job and do so with the truth as your basis, which I took seriously.

But why not Advertising or Marketing? Well, to be honest, I am not a natural salesperson, and if you know anything about Marketing and Advertising, both are tied directly to the bottom line. It was not a good fit for me to have to create a tagline to *sell* or design something to motivate a purchase. At the end of the day, I wanted to build relationships, write with a purpose, and help people share their stories through the various media channels.

Public Relations offers the widest array of opportunities. A skilled PR practitioner can work in any field from government to entertainment, politics to activism, nonprofits to corporations or agencies with specialties or those with clients in a wide range of industries. I tell my students that if you have the ability to write well and build genuine relationships, tap into what makes a company special in its industry, and be persuasive through the use of research, then you have a solid basis for success.

CONVERTING SKILLS TO PRACTICAL APPLICATION

Not all students who major in PR expect to be practitioners. But every skill a student acquires can stay with them throughout whatever career they chose to pursue. Even if you think you know what you want to do with the rest of your life, never turn down the opportunity to gain a new skill or sharpen one you have.

Students studying PR should approach each new skill as a new tool to add to their tool box. It's not something you drop in and never touch again, but something you practice with so that your skills stay sharp and you stay adept, because you never know when you will need to use it. Creating a PR Campaign is a college class that should allow students to take their toolbox and challenge them to utilize every single tool and skill they have acquired throughout their college career in the application of one project that has so many moving parts and levels to it that it takes teams to create a quality PR Campaign.

Any student who comes into a PR Campaigns class of mine and says, "I think I could do this on my own, I don't work well in teams" is someone whose success in the business world I worry about. I say to that student that perhaps they have mastered the writing, design, research, and even business writing components of the campaign, but the challenge for them is to master the teamwork aspect. Every person on a team has their own set of amazing skills that are fine-tuned and polished, and every person has something they can work on before they begin their professional career. For most students taking this course as a senior in a capstone, this is your final chance to work out the kinks and get yourself to where you are your BEST SELF.

My mentor was Cal Sutliff, whose book *The Power of YOUR People Skills* is something I use in conjunction with all the worksheets and handouts you are about to have at your fingertips. I use his book not because he was my mentor or I wanted to sell his book but because I wanted my students to understand that to be the best teammate and to create something that is as big and as momentous as what you are about to create, it takes you contributing YOUR best work and being the best teammate YOU can be.

APPENDIX

The Appendix (page 143) is a sample PR Campaign for the DJ Irie Foundation, which was completed by my students in fall 2017 as an assignment for the Public Relations campaigns class. The purpose of including a real PR Campaign is to provide an example of one continuous campaign to use as a reference. Again, final PR Campaigns are tailored to the specific client, so each one is unique. Although the full PR Campaign for the DJ Irie Foundation was more than 400 pages, the author and publishers opted to select the most relevant sections to provide the user with a basic understanding of the concepts and steps that are explained in the text.

FINAL NOTES

Use what is in this book as a guideline and a basis for what is necessary and build from there. For every class I've ever had, I challenged to add their own special *flavor* to create something for the client that wasn't prescribed. When you aim for the bare minimum, that is what you achieve, but when you reach for the stars, I promise you all will achieve more than you knew you could.

As you move your way through the creation of the campaign, here are the questions I ask my students, which I remind them of often:

- Have you dug deep and really looked at this from every angle?

- Are you carefully phrasing what you are writing to be clear and to be honest, but also to be *kind* to the client?

- Are you playing the *what if* game when you write?

- Are you staying true to AP Style, the organization's brand, and the class's style?

- Is your idea plausible within the timeline and budget the client has given to us?

- Is this predictable and tired or something that is innovative and different?

- Are you looking backward and forward to gain perspective? You need to look both ways before you cross a street, right?

ACKNOWLEDGMENTS

It is only fitting to begin the acknowledgments of *The PR Campaigns Worktext* by specifically thanking the students I have had throughout my more than a decade in teaching this course at the elite college level. Every single class inspired me to tweak the curriculum, find new ways to allow students to have creative freedom, and inspire the PR practitioners of the future to push themselves to achieve their best possible work.

PR Campaigns is often the capstone class, and that means it is the moment in which students get to apply all they have learned and pour their hearts and souls into projects that demonstrate their professional capabilities to the world, to themselves, to their parents, and to the client. So again, to the students who have challenged, inspired, motivated, and taught me in the past, I simply cannot thank you enough. To the students I will have in the future, I hope this guides you through successful professional practices for many years.

PR Campaigns are only as strong as the clients who are willing to work with us, so it's important for me to thank organizations such as Comic Cure, Florida Panthers Foundation, Gridiron Grill-Off, Hard Rock Energy, Miami Open, PGA Tour, and countless others for allowing the students to learn from you and create something for you.

A special acknowledgement in this *PR Campaigns Worktext* must be given to Shobie Callahan and the Irie Foundation for partnering with the class to create a PR Campaign for Irie Weekend and Irie Foundation. The work of Kaitlyn Hopkins and Krizia Mendez is featured as a stellar example of what students can create.

Professionally, when I started teaching Public Relations, Dr. Cornelia Splichal was always the most supportive of my teaching efforts and my methods for PR Campaigns and served as a wonderful mentor to me. Additionally, I would be lost if it wasn't for the friendship and guidance of Dr. Shannon Campbell, who is not only brilliant and a gifted academic but also a well-rounded practitioner and a wonderful friend and colleague. I would also like to posthumously recognize my mentor Cal Sutliff, who helped me on my journey to be the best version of myself and who always believed in my efforts as an educator and mentor to others. I would be remiss if I didn't acknowledge the advice, guidance, and support I received from: Professor Cathryn Edelstein (Senior Executive-in-Residence, Emerson College), Dr. Philip Glenn (Professor, Emerson College), Professor Jack Miller (Professor of Practice, University of Miami), Dr. Diane Millette (Chair, University of Miami), Dr. Greg Payne (Chair, Emerson College), Dr. Don Stacks (University of Miami, Retired), and Dr. Richard West (Professor, Emerson College).

I'd like to thank all the people who reviewed drafts of this book: Michelle Groover, Georgia Southern University; Jamie Ward, Eastern Michigan University; Victoria Brodie, California Baptist University; Dr. Christina Paxman, Minot State University; Dr. Candice Lanius, University of Alabama in Huntsville; Hazel J. Cole, University of West Georgia; Dr. Arshia Anwer, Manhattan College; Kurt Wise, University of West Florida; Carol Osborne, University of South Florida; Ilwoo Ju, Purdue University; Shannon B. Campbell, Metropolitan State University of Denver; and Lisa Du Bois Low, Texas Tech University.

Finally, I would not have achieved the success in my professional or academic careers if it wasn't for the guidance and support I had growing up. To my mother, Pamela Elles, who is not only the best educator and administrator I've ever known but who also is a wonderful editor and is the best mother I could ever have hoped for—thank you. You gave me the gift of travel and enlightenment and taught me that I could do anything I put my mind to. Thank you also to grandparents who were instrumental in raising me and to my extended family in Tampa and the women who have become like sisters to me throughout my life. Your support has always been appreciated.

ABOUT THE AUTHOR

Maria Elles Scott, Assistant Professor at Emerson College, teaches Public Relations and Sports Communication courses in both the undergraduate and graduate programs. Dr. Scott comes with more than 10 years of teaching experience and more than 20 years of experience as a journalist and Public Relations professional. As an academic, Dr. Scott started her full-time teaching career in 2007 at the University of Miami, where she began applying her real-world experience to the classroom. Dr. Scott has taught more than 250 students how to create a full Public Relations Campaign for clients that include PGA Tour, NHL Florida Panthers Foundation, Red Bull, Hard Rock Energy Drink, Irie Foundation, Miami Open, St. Jude Children's Research Hospital, Jason Taylor Foundation, and so many more. Additionally, Dr. Scott taught Advanced Public Relations Messaging, where students created a full media kit for a client, a graduate graphics design course, and the Public Relations Experience Program.

In her professional career, Dr. Scott started at 20 years old as a sports journalist with the *Tampa Tribune* before she moved to the Philadelphia area and the Journal Register Company. Dr. Scott transitioned into Public Relations working for the Tampa Bay Super Bowl XXXV Task Force before moving to ESPN where she was the publicity and community relations specialist for all ESPN event properties, such as the X Games, Winter X Games, and ESPY Awards. Dr. Scott moved from Los Angeles to South Florida, where she managed Public Relations for the Miami Open and then moved to the South Florida Super Bowl XLI Host Committee. In 2007, Dr. Scott opened her own consulting firm while teaching full time. Dr. Scott has assisted with events and publicity for Michael Irvin's PlayMaker Charities and Foundation, Battle of the Beauties, Sports Employment Inc., Dwight Stephenson Foundation, and the National Salute to America's Heroes presented by Hyundai.

In her professional career, Dr. Scott created two campaigns in conjunction with the NFL as part of the Super Bowl Host Committee in 2001 and 2007. She developed the plan to deploy a community-wide *pride* program to recruit volunteers for the Super Bowl in Tampa (2001) and South Florida (2007). While at ESPN, she worked with the central marketing department to create grassroots campaigns in Philadelphia and Los Angeles to engage the target audience in the X Games.

Since joining the Emerson College family as the Public Relations Faculty Program Coordinator, Scott has worked with Emerson Launch and Voice @ Emerson as well as her students to create and launch Voicelets on the Amazon Alexa platform as a voice component to the curriculum. Additionally, in Fall 2018, she became the Emerson College Chapter Public Relations Student Society of America Chapter Faculty Advisory.

CHAPTER 1

GETTING STARTED

CAMPAIGNS

What Is a PR Campaign?

Examples of Public Relations (PR) campaigns are traced back to medieval times, periods throughout history with religious wars, times when new countries and governments were emerging. Campaigns have always been a way to inform and persuade the masses. Specifically, in the United States, examples of campaigns are well documented beginning in the 1700s and 1800s as the United States was positioning itself on the world's stage, creating alliances and harnessing its own people to work is a collective against a common enemy. During the Revolutionary War, there are many who believe that the actions of Samuel Adams were strategically set to position the British in a poor light using terms like *Boston Massacre* and disseminating information to the public with a clear agenda.

Public Relations *campaigns* as we know them today have been around since the creation of modern PR practice, which began at the start of the 1900s. Historic figures in PR such as Edward Bernays, Ivy Lee and Betsy Plank all influenced how modern PR campaigns are conducted. In the 1998 biography of Edward Bernays by *Boston Globe* reporter Larry Tye titled "The Father of Spin," Bernays' career and accomplishments are well documented. In addition to creating an outline for propaganda techniques, ethics for practitioners and more, Bernays was very influential in creating the eight-step process to create a Public Relations plan on which most campaigns are loosely based. This process includes Objectives, Situation, Strategy, Audience, Tactics, Timeline and/or Calendar, Budget and Evaluation.

Modern PR campaigns present solutions to one goal. Throughout history, these *goals* often helped change the ideas of war, persuade the masses, build brands, impact outcomes, start movements, end conflicts and much more. Broken down into measurable objectives, the tactics used to create successful campaigns are skills practitioners constantly fine-tune.

A Public Relations Campaign Is:

- A PR campaign is a communication plan—a strategically chosen set of various communication media platforms—that seek to influence a specific target audience or audiences. Communication plans are simple, cohesive, power pieces of persuasion. They *build a case* on facts and insights that demonstrate to a client *why* the course chosen is the correct one to yield the desired results to the target audience.

- A PR campaign is conducted to solve a problem or take advantage of an opportunity. The issue solved or opportunity gained must benefit both the organization and the public—meaning it's a *win-win*. The implication is that if the resulting situation is a *win-lose*, the outcome is often *lose-lose*. In other words, an organization is not likely to thrive long term without listening to and serving its public, both internal (employees, stakeholders, board of trustees, volunteers) and external (clients, customers, members) in the short term.

A Public Relations Campaign Is Not:

- A PR campaign is not an advertising *blitz*. Advertising is frequently associated with the word campaign, but remember that advertising is usually PAID. The PR campaign employs many methods of communication including media relations (utilizing tactical PR writing such as media advisories, media alerts, media pitches, press releases, etc.), social media, publicity and other methods, all of which are not paid forms of media. An effective PR campaign typically utilizes a range of traditional and non-traditional media and employs influence by opinion leaders and the community.

- A PR campaign is not blind propaganda. In modern political discourse, there is almost always an underlying thread of propaganda and influence of mass audiences. Propaganda, at its core practice, relies on generalizing the appeal to the audience evoking collective emotions, is often devoid of facts, evidence, or reality and relies on defamation. PR campaigns require credible facts that the public can understand, evaluate and utilize. The target audience is free to choose and accept the information and therefore act or deny the information. The success of the persuasion is based on action or inaction.

- A PR campaign is not spin or hype. *Spin* usually refers to efforts to tilt the public perception in ways favorable to a political candidate or product. Unfortunately, it has a negative connotation and is often synonymous with the practice of PR. When used, spin usually means the twisting of the truth to only highlight the positive and "dizzy" the audience. The term *hype* is derived from *hyperbole*, which is an exaggeration to impress and evoke a strong response. No legitimate PR campaign achieves successful goals and hits the marks with the objectives using spin or hype. Do successful campaigns based in hype exist? Of course. But it's important to differentiate that in the age of digital information, flash and buzz do not create a long-term lasting campaign. Weak arguments and tools aiming to just bewilder or bedazzle are not going create a lasting impression that has measureable results in the long-term. What practitioners often see is *glitz* and *buzz* are often followed by nay-sayers and contradiction, which puts the client in the center of confusion or worse a cloud of controversy and ultimately never leads to success.

- A PR campaign is also not a PR program for a company. A PR program is a long-term strategy that should incorporate the ethics of an organization, strategies for rolling-out new information, handling a crisis and sticking to a brand. Within a PR program, a company can often have one or several PR campaigns a year for various reasons—ultimately to achieve a goal. An example of this is M&M-Mars refreshing its brand in the 1990s and inviting the public to pick a new color for an M&M. The public voted to remove the tan M&M and create a blue M&M. This was an extremely successful campaign for the brand and led to another global search for a new color—purple in 2002; M&Ms characters in 2007; and in 2010 personalized M&Ms.

Types of Campaigns

What brings about a campaign in the first place? It is often the desire for change or the result of a needed resolution after an issue or problem comes to public light. These are marvelous opportunities to advance the organization. Some changes are sweeping and incorporate thousands of people, such as the suffrage movement in the 1920s to approve the amendment to the U.S. Constitution giving women the right to vote. The spark can ignite a fire or a flame; either way, all PR campaigns follow a similar path from inception to execution.

Before any of the PR campaign is created, it's imperative that everyone understands what type of campaign is being built. The most common categories for persuasive PR campaigns are commercial, educational, political, reputation and social change.

Commercial campaigns roll out a new product or service for sale to the public, or it revitalizes awareness of existing products or services. PR campaigns can precede an advertising blitz through media channels. The PR campaign often educates the public to the product and/or service and informs members of the public of key words needed to discuss this product and/or service properly. At the time of the launch, the public already understands the term *smart phone* as opposed to *cellular phone* and the differences. The public knows what a *touch screen* means and has already had their concerns recognized and addressed through the PR campaign messaging. By this point, all the advertisers have to focus on is the cost and where to purchase the product. Commercial PR campaigns create tactical PR materials, pitches, demonstrations, events and trials for the press to deliver third-party reviews and analysis of the product and/or service.

> *Example:* In September 2009 Starbucks broke successfully into the $21 billion global instant coffee business by introducing *VIA* within the cafes. This was rapidly followed by pep-rallies, a cocktail mix-off, a nationwide road trip, taste tests and much more, including PR materials educating the public on *ethically sourced* products.

Educational or *informational* PR campaigns seek to raise public awareness of issues, organizations, products, or services. These are also known as *public awareness campaigns* due to the level of awareness it offers on a specific subject. These campaigns are often utilized by nonprofit organizations to help people better understand, relate and activate. Most of the public has a loose understanding of the term *learning disabled*. But through a PR campaign, an organization can work to replace harmful words used in spoken lexicon, explain the various types of disabilities and shift attitudes and behaviors. These are among the most common type of PR campaign because elements of education and/or information exist in ALL PR campaigns—efforts to help people better comprehend the underlying causes and how that might connect to their beliefs and so on.

> *Example:* In 2010, the U.S. government began nationwide educational initiatives to combat the rise in incidents related to bullying: National Bullying Prevention Campaign. The Health Resources and Services Administration (HRSA) Maternal and Child Health Bureau targets tweens—those ages 9 to 13 years of age—and the adults who are responsible for these tweens. The multiyear PR campaign included bullying prevention resource kits, a national launch event, advice for young people, PSAs, a website filled with data and other materials and more. The campaign used animated characters to depict bullying scenarios in entertaining *webisodes* and PSAs. The Substance Abuse and Mental Health Services Administration (SAMHSA) launched a parallel PR campaign driving home to parents that it only

takes 15 minutes of time talking and listening a day to have a positive effect on behavior. The PR campaign raised awareness, recommended action and created talking points for parents to start conversation and red flags for them to watch for to prevent bullying behaviors or outcomes.

Political campaigns are something of a horse of a different color in that most of these are either focused on the candidate or the issues and then have an element of persuasion, education and/or information and salesmanship layered on top of the base. Political campaigns are best when handled by a team of people, which includes a PR expert, but where strategy and political connections and/or adeptness are equally important. The candidate's ability to appear capable, relatable and genuine seems to be crucial to the voters with the integration of various mediums that are largely on 24-hour news cycles. People are able to obtain information from these sources with little-to-no understanding of validity of facts.

Reputation PR campaigns center on a *brand* and aim to change the reputation of that brand through a series of strategic messages, PR stunts, positive press, social media banter and more. Not all reputation PR campaigns are aimed to *polish* a tarnished reputation. Some are created to breathe life into a wilting brand, shift the demographics of a once-loved but forgotten brand, or realign the values of a brand. Reputation PR campaigns are often best used for well-established organizations and are also interested in long-term results. It is implausible to believe that reputation adjustments are made in short spans of time; rather, it is more likely that these campaigns have steps measures.

Example: In 2014, the relatively *young* brand of Air B&B launched a reputation PR campaign introducing *The Bélo*, which asked users to interpret the logo or symbol by adding colors, decorations, backgrounds and so on. The brand wanted users to interpret the symbol to something meaningful to them, which is a way to connect the brand to each user. This moved the user base from those who viewed Air B&B from the youth-based market to something for *everyone*, which was not part of the reputation the brand had previously.

Social change PR campaigns are movement-based and are aimed to target large segments of the public and push for something *bigger*. Social change PR campaigns often incorporate large percentages of education and information-based PR campaigns. Most of social change is compelling a person or groups of people to take action, it also requires that the person or group of people *believe* to some extent in the action they are taking. It is difficult to harness thousands of people to march against ___ for the right to ___ if that group of people doesn't believe in what they are literally marching for. Social change PR campaigns are unique in that they can be quick and from inception to execution can happen in 60 days or they can be something that builds for years.

Example: In January 2017, the Women's March was a worldwide protest in Washington, D.C., held the day after the inauguration of President Donald Trump. During the campaign, tensions rose following statements made by Trump and his camp that many considered to be anti-women and offensive. The Women's March on Washington was streamed live on social media platforms and drew more than 200,000 people to the nation's capital. Other marches were held worldwide and in cities throughout the United States with an approximate total of more than 4 million people participating in marches. It was the largest single-day protest in U.S. history.

TEAMWORK

Working in Teams

Throughout college campuses and within the business world, the word *teamwork* usually evokes fear, panic and frustration. At minimum, it strikes a negative connotation. The reality, however, is that in the modern workforce, teamwork is collective thinking models and shared workloads is more common than ever before. Employers are moving further from the traditional or formal organizational structure of the pyramid hierarchy in lieu of a more horizontal structure. Changing the perception of the teamwork or group work begins with explaining the process and choosing a team or group configuration that maximizes the labor force and optimizes time and resources by playing to strengths.

The Real World

In PR, the ability to create, plan, implement and evaluate a campaign is the cornerstone of your skills. Regardless of the industry in which you work, it is unlikely you will ever develop a complete campaign alone. It is more common that you will be asked to work in a team or even lead the team.

The campaign process is such that it is divided and split any number of ways to share the work equally, capitalizing on talents and/or strengths and pooling resources. When working in a classroom environment, the instructor may choose a less conventional method of dividing labor or may opt to have the students select teams or groups themselves. The latter situation can lead teams that are not well balanced, but are comprised of teams of friends.

The Division of Labor

For the purposes of this worktext, I have opted to proceed as if students are working in two or more teams or groups to complete a full PR campaign within a semester or trimester. As such, I have provided a few steps and options to assist the course instructor or professor or team leader in dividing labor and responsibilities. This process lays the groundwork for teamwork in the course.

Step One

The first step is to identify the strengths of each class member. This can be accomplished in a number of ways, but if time is of the essence, an easy way is to bring in copies of past classwork and assignments to compare and contrast with a universal or classwide scale to quantify each student's abilities. If the university or college offers an upper division writing or publications course, the materials created in this class are the suggested examples to use for this process. The simplest way for the professor to judge the work is to use a grading rubric looking for:

- AP style
- Clarity and/or brevity
- Content and delivery
- Paragraph structure and transitions
- Proper use of formatting
- Spelling, grammar and punctuation

Another option is to have the faculty member assign the teams within the first two meetings. This allows the instructor the chance to gauge strengths and weaknesses and team dynamics (personalities). A final option is to select team leaders and then allow the selected students to pick the rest of their teams. I do not recommend this option because it often results in teams based on friendships, popularity, or perceived *smarts* or good grades. It is also unrealistic because in the workforce, teams are rarely selected by the team leader.

Step Two

The second step is to determine *how* the class is to accomplish all the tasks needed to create a campaign efficiently. This translates into determining if teams are sufficient or whether groups should be added to further divide tasks and responsibilities.

For a large class (15 or more students), it is possible that creating three teams of five students each is enough to accomplish a full campaign within a semester—assuming each team has a different *focus*, such as a different target audience or objective. In this option, each team produces an entire campaign proposal or plan, instead of working with the other teams to create one overall campaign. The result is that the client receives three different campaign proposals or plans. This might be ideal for some clients who wish to have ideas to choose from. Many times, the resulting work from the *competing* campaign groups' or teams' strategy is that the teams push each other to think outside the box and to push the other team and/or competition.

For a smaller class, or in a PR agency environment, I suggest a blended or multi-layer option that combines the use of both teams or groups and *division*. In this model, the team or group has an individual focus (such as the target audience, outcome, etc.) and divisions are divided by function (i.e., writing tactical, graphic design, research, etc.). Using this option allows students to work together across teams in creating one unified plan; it is especially attractive because they are exposed to more students' collaboration, ideas and talents.

Examples of teams:

Team A: Target Audience is Millennials

Bobby (Tactical Writer)

Maritza (Graphic Designer)

Marquis (Researcher)

Tamara (Plan Writer)

Team B: Target Audience is Generation X

Aimee (Graphic Designer)

Jake (Researcher)

Kenneth (Plan Writer)

Theresa (Tactical Writer)

Team C: Target Audience is Baby Boomers

Alexa (Researcher)

Cristeena (Plan Writer)

Kale (Graphic Designer)

Yvette (Tactical Writer)

WORKSHEET 1A

PR CAMPAIGN BASICS

Before a PR agency or a PR *class* delves into creating a PR campaign, it is important to determine what type of PR campaign you are creating.

From the worktext, the most common categories for persuasive PR campaigns are commercial, educational, political, reputation and social change. Using the definitions and examples provided, what type do you believe is best for this client?

_____

_____

_____

_____

_____

_____

_____

_____

Why do you believe this is the type of campaign you are creating? Support your answer above with your thinking.

_____

_____

_____

_____

_____

_____

_____

_____

_____

Why is it NOT possible that the campaign is one of the other types?

_____

_____

_____

_____

_____

_____

_____

_____

_____

It's common to jump directly to assuming that a campaign is an educational or informational campaign. Since so many PR campaigns are this type of PR campaign, ask yourself the following questions:

- What information would you need to disseminate?
- What does the public need to be educated about?
- How does information help the public activate?
- What education and/or information leads to activation in a meaningful way?
- How can you inform and/or educate the media and how does that impact your campaign?

WORKSHEET 1B

TEAMMATES

Part I: Dividing into teams.

Start by identifying your own strengths (as a person):

_____

_____

_____

_____

_____

_____

_____

_____

_____

Circle what you feel are your strengths as a PR Practitioner:

Graphic Design Research   (Social Media)   Writing (Plan)   Writing (Tactical)

*In this model, everyone has a part in the overall strategy.

Part II: Being the best teammate YOU can be.

Start by identifying your own hot buttons. According to Cal Sutliff in *The Power of YOUR People Skills*, hot buttons are your personal triggers that elicit an automatic and exaggerated response that is uncontrollable. What are your hot buttons?

_____

_____

_____

_____

_____

_____

_____

_____

_____

List what you believe makes you a good teammate:

_____

_____

_____

_____

_____

_____

_____

_____

List what you look for in a good teammate to BALANCE what you bring to a team:

_____

_____

_____

_____

_____

_____

_____

_____

_____

List what you believe is the WORST thing your teammate could do to you:

_____

_____

_____

_____

_____

_____

_____

_____

_____

Part III: Communication keys to team-based discussions.

Once you know your hot buttons, what makes you a good teammate, what you look for and what brings balance, you all need to focus on laying the groundwork for a strong communication plan.

Circle the terms you believe are essential to open communication in a team:

(Honesty)   Integrity   (Access)   Sharing   (Respect)   Balance

Conflict often reduces the ability to communicate. List one GOOD and one BAD communication habit you have that leads to conflict:

_____

_____

_____

_____

Communicating in a team-based environment can be challenging. Most people feel it is hard to *manage* a lot of personalities without upsetting any one person. The reality is that instead of focusing on how to manage others, most people just need to learn how to manage their own communication interactions.

As a communicator in a team, are you a leader or follower? _leader_

Are you aggressive, assertive, or passive? _Assertive_

When confronted with a conflict, do you get defensive or submissive? _Submissive_

"I" statements are the best way for you to communicate your own feelings with others, especially in a conflict. It eliminates blame and reduces confrontation. Change the following examples into "I" statements.

"YOU" Statements	"I" Statements

You did the research all wrong.

You have missed every deadline.

You are the main issue we are having.

Your tardiness has caused our team this issue.

Part IV: People skills are a life-long lesson.

A lot of why people do not like working in teams is that it forces them to confront their own weaknesses (usually pointed out by others). People who approach perfecting their people skills as a life-long lesson usually have a more fluid idea that they are always a *work in progress*.

What are some issues you've faced working in teams in the past you wish to resolve with this project?

_____

_____

_____

_____

_____

_____

_____

_____

What do you feel is your biggest challenge working in teams? How do you plan to tackle it?

_____

_____

_____

_____

_____

_____

What takeaways have you already mastered from previous experiences that make you a better teammate today?

_____

_____

_____

_____

_____

_____

Your life-long journey begins with this project. This will be stressful and bring out your hot buttons. How do you plan to prevent your hot buttons from harming your team and/or teammates?

_____

_____

_____

_____

_____

_____

_____

CHAPTER 2

CLIENT MEETING QUESTIONS AND NOTES

WORKING WITH *REAL* CLIENTS

Creating a Campaign for a Class

Public Relations campaigns classes have been part of curriculum for more than 80 years at college programs through the United States and abroad. Many of these courses were taught as a survey of ideas or examination of case studies reviewing successful campaigns completed by agencies and corporate teams.

Even PR practitioners who are internal to a corporation must still have a *client meeting* with the department or group with whom they are partnering to create a campaign. Before anyone can start to identify the issue, create a goal statement, craft objectives, outline a research plan and examine the target audience, everything begins with the initial client meetings. Externally, agencies use this initial meeting to cover a lot of ground, not just to review the elements of the campaign, but also to delve into the company through a situation analysis and more.

Meeting with the client and/or department is part of a two-way communication model in that the agency or company team has to provide a sense of professionalism and knowledge to earn the trust of the client and/or department. The internal and external piece is an important step and an essential skill to master and fine-tune no matter how many campaigns a person has completed.

Setting Up the Meeting

It is important to set the ground rules before the meeting begins. The agency and/or company team must be clear to set a baseline for how communication will flow, how and when decisions are made and how questions are asked and answered. The first two meetings should alternate between locations where the company and the team share information and resources.

It is best to have a meeting when all parties are ready to discuss the project, in the right mindset and ready to begin moving forward. It is important for the company to understand that the campaign is a complex project with many moving parts, which means that the development of the plan is only as strong as the information that is contributed by the client, company, or department and the needs that are communicated. This process of initial discussions must be open and honest. Ethically, the team and/or agency should be clear in their explanation that while they can create a comprehensive campaign with research to support their decisions, it is up to the public to interact and react with the messaging and the client, company, or department to follow the plan and not deviate or add any additional elements (like a crisis).

Ethics in Public Relations

Ethics are defined as the moral base that governs a person's behaviors and/or the ways in which a person makes decisions and takes action. Within the field of Public Relations, a practitioner must apply their own person ethics within their decision-making process. Additionally, a practitioner must take into account the ethics of their company if they work for an agency and most important, they must consider the ethics of the client. I suggest at this stage that it is imperative to have an important conversation with your client about their values and their ethics. Many times, a company has an ethical standard or practices if it interacts with the public in any way.

Ethics are interpreted loosely and because each person has their own set of ethics, it is challenging to find a common ground when people approach the conversation from a broad approach. I suggest the best way to approach a rational and productive discussion on setting your own code of ethics for the project is to begin with the very basic elements that impact most communication projects such as use of imagery, use of shared information, historic documentation, attribution and credit and more. It's not uncommon to then incorporate the code of ethics or ethical standards from the company.

Example: An organization that works with children might have a standard of ethics that includes that all adults working in direct contact with children are subjected to a background check and annual mandatory training. Additionally, the code of ethics might dictate that parents only pickup their only children and follow similar standards to schools.

The Public Relations Society of America (PRSA) offers members a set of professional guidelines and code of ethics to follow in their professional career. The International Public Relations Association (IPRA) offers members a code of conduct that guides their professional actions and offers clarity of actions. Both the PRSA and IPRA codes are seen as core guidelines in the PR field and are used as guidelines for professionals as well as taught in college courses.

THE INTERNATIONAL PUBLIC RELATIONS ASSOCIATION CODE OF CONDUCT

The IPRA Code of Conduct

Adopted in 2011, the IPRA Code of Conduct is an affirmation of professional and ethical conduct by members of the International Public Relations Association and recommended to public relations practitioners worldwide.

In the conduct of public relations practitioners shall:

1. Observance
   Observe the principles of the UN Charter and the Universal Declaration of Human Rights;

2. Integrity
Act with honesty and integrity at all times so as to secure and retain the confidence of those with whom the practitioner comes into contact;

3. Dialogue
Seek to establish the moral, cultural and intellectual conditions for dialogue, and recognize the rights of all parties involved to state their case and express their views;

4. Transparency
Be open and transparent in declaring their name, organization and the interest they represent;

5. Conflict
Avoid any professional conflicts of interest and to disclose such conflicts to affected parties when they occur;

6. Confidentiality
Honor confidential information provided to them;

7. Accuracy
Take all reasonable steps to ensure the truth and accuracy of all information provided;

8. Falsehood
Make every effort to not intentionally disseminate false or misleading information, exercise proper care to avoid doing so unintentionally and correct any such act promptly;

9. Deception
Not obtain information by deceptive or dishonest means;

10. Disclosure
Not create or use any organization to serve an announced cause but which actually serves an undisclosed interest;

11. Profit
Not sell for profit to third parties copies of documents obtained from public authorities;

12. Remuneration
Whilst providing professional services, not accept any form of payment in connection with those services from anyone other than the principal;

13. Inducement
Neither directly nor indirectly offer nor give any financial or other inducement to public representatives or the media, or other stakeholders;

14. Influence
Neither propose nor undertake any action which would constitute an improper influence on public representatives, the media, or other stakeholders;

15. Competitors
Not intentionally injure the professional reputation of another practitioner;

16. Poaching
Not seek to secure another practitioner's client by deceptive means;

17. Employment
When employing personnel from public authorities or competitors take care to follow the rules and confidentiality requirements of those organizations;

18. Colleagues
Observe this Code with respect to fellow IPRA members and public relations practitioners worldwide.

IPRA members shall, in upholding this Code, agree to abide by and help enforce the disciplinary procedures of the International Public Relations Association in regard to any breach of this Code.

Credit: By kind permission of the International Public Relations Association. www.ipra.org IPRA — leading trust and ethics in global communication

Taking Notes

Many young people take notes based on their days in classrooms. These notes are very different than the notes needed to detail the happenings of business meetings. Best practice in running a meeting is to start with an agenda; this provides structure to the meeting and hopefully prevents derailment. The notes should be organized to parallel the agenda, utilizing the same bullet points, levels and order.

One person per team should be designated to take notes. Within each section, the note-taker should be careful to make a list of action items and *assign* any follow-up tasks. The most efficient way to do this is by using initials in the notes. Be careful if multiple people are taking notes from computers using Google Docs or another shared system that the people don't write over each other and so on.

Notes should not only be about what is said in the meeting, but other observations as well. If there is a team of people present, designate another person to take paper notes or computer notes on any other observations such as body language, facial expressions, changes in breathing, eye contact and more. These observations can often lead to a deeper understanding of the greater issues and more.

Asking the Right Questions

During the first and second meeting between the client, company, or department and the team, it is best practice to create a list of questions prior to starting and putting the answers to those questions next to what is proposed. As the meeting progresses, there may be a number of questions that will go unanswered.

Preface questions about their personal view of the company by using terms such as *from your viewpoint* or *based on your perspective* and then ask the question. Many times, if you come right out and ask, "What do you think is the issue?" there might not be a clear answer from the entire team. On the other hand, the bid for the project may have included the issue, but that is as far as the client, company, or department got and did not go beyond.

Good Questions:

- Can you share with us some examples of campaigns or plans that have, in your opinion, been successful at reaching your target audience, delivering the message and getting them to activate? Please explain why your team believes this was a success.

- Can you share with us some examples of campaigns or plans that have, in your opinion, been unsuccessful at reaching your target audience, delivering the message and getting them to activate? Please explain why your team believes they were not a success.

- How does the company and/or department believe it is perceived within the community and the public?

Bad Questions:

- How would you solve this problem?

- What would you like to repeat?

- Why did you stop working with other companies?

- Why aren't you successful?

Answering the Right Questions

When the client, company, or department asks questions of the campaigns team, it is important for the team to be honest and ethical, which means not overselling or promising to deliver what you are unable to do. Since it is difficult to gauge what types of questions you might be asked, you have to prepare the team for any type of question that might arise.

Good Answers:

- The campaign plan our team prepares includes a calendar of when to deploy the tactics and the evaluations and measurements to ensure that each of the tactics provided are successful.

- The PR campaign for your client, company, or department is aimed at the target audience and has messaging tailored specifically to this audience.

- The execution of the campaign is in the hands of both the client, company, or department and the campaign team. In teamwork, both sides have to contribute to make the campaign a success.

Bad Answers:

- The campaign team did our part, now it's up to you so; if it fails, it's your fault.

- The content is good; maybe the audience just doesn't get it or like the client, company, or department.

WORKSHEET 2A

CLIENT MEETING

GETTING ORGANIZED:

Date and Time:

Location:

Attendees:

Agenda:

QUESTIONS FOR THE CLIENT, COMPANY, OR DEPARTMENT:

What are some of the questions you think need to be answered (refer to the list of good questions above)? Right one question per line and number each question.

Ex: 1. How have you measured success on your campaigns in the past?

_____

_____

_____

_____

_____

_____

_____

_____

_____

_____

_____

_____

_____

What are some of the observations your team has made about the client? What body language does the client exhibit? Are there moments when the client seems more interested or engaged than others? Some body language to consider: eye contact, facial expressions, arms crossed, head nods and so on.

_____

_____

_____

_____

_____

_____

_____

_____

_____

_____

_____

OTHER QUESTIONS TO CONSIDER:

- What are some of the reasons the client, company, or department has engaged successfully with the audience in the past?

_____

_____

_____

- What are some meaningful words or phrases the audiences responds to?

  _____

  _____

  _____

- Does the client, company, or department understand their situation analysis?

  _____

  _____

  _____

- Does the client, company, or department already speak to the target audience?

  _____

  _____

  _____

- Historically, how has the client, company, or department handled a crisis?

  _____

  _____

  _____

- Does the company have a solid plan for handling conflict before it becomes a crisis?

  _____

  _____

  _____

- What audiences does the client, company, or department miss?

  _____

  _____

  _____

- What other missed opportunities are out there that can be handled in this campaign?

_____

_____

_____

Add more questions here:

_____

_____

_____

_____

_____

_____

_____

_____

_____

_____

_____

WORKSHEET 2B

ETHICAL STANDARDS

ORGANIZATION'S CODE OF ETHICS:

1) Honesty
2) Loyalty
3) Fairness
4) Advocacy

What other ethical standards are important to the organization?

- Justice /accountability
-

What are your OWN personal ethical standards?

- Honesty
- Transparency
- Fairness

Ethically, how do you feel about the following;

- Using images off the internet? — Nay; transparent images
- Using images off of social media? — yes if its our specific account
- Using information off the internet? — Only from our own research
- Using information off social media? — "
- Assigning proper credit or attribution to contributors and/or creators?
- Interaction on social media? — yes!
- Cooperation with partners? Sharing information?

Add your own here:

CHAPTER 3

DEFINING THE *PROJECT*

WRITING THE ISSUE AND GOAL STATEMENTS

Where to Begin?

Especially for students, creating the tactical elements and strategy are always the most *fun* and there is usually a rush to jump in and get started on creating materials for the client. Beginning with meeting the client, students must start to gather *clues* to determine the nature of the overall project.

Many times, a client or company many believe it knows what its issue is and how to resolve it. In some cases, a PR campaign is the result of a failed attempt to deploy a strategy.

> *Example:* If a company feels like the reason its nonprofit arm is not gaining the traction it deserves amongst its core audience, it will create more visible marketing materials with obvious calls to action. When that also fails to elicit more support, the company many then turn to a PR campaign to determine the issue, analyze the situation, research and create a strategy and then a full campaign.

Writing the Issue Statement

Issue statements are usually one sentence and are a summation of the overarching problem faced by the company and/or client that the campaign centers on resolving. This is determined after conversations with the client and, many times, a full analysis of the situation. The situation analysis is a detailed examination of the company and/or client from a number of viewpoints and includes the creation of a SWOT (Strengths, Weaknesses, Opportunities, Threats).

The issue statement is created by breaking down a few key factors and finessing the phrasing in such a way that results in a clear, concise, direct and focused statement that is easy to comprehend and directly connected to the goal statement.

Example of a broken-down issue statement:

> The issue for _____ (client) is a lack of _____ (issue—i.e., awareness, information, understanding, activation) by the target audience of _____ (target audience) on the subjects of _____, _____, _____ and _____ (focus of the issue).

> The issue for the DJ Irie Foundation is a lack of awareness and therefore under-standing by the target audience of Miami-Dade County youth and their parents or caregivers on the programs offered afterschool and the enrichment offered to them in the areas of music, dance and the creative arts (See Appendix Page 146).

Refining Your Statement

The worksheet helps you refine your own statement. Once you draft your statement, it takes discussions with the company and/or client and your own team to discuss not only the word choice, but also the path you are embarking on. The ideal issue statement is neither negative nor is it biased. A talented writer is capable of writing a statement demonstrating the need for improvement in areas of weakness.

Writing the Goal Statement

The goal is often confused with objectives and these are not interchangeable terms. A goal statement is the broader and overarching results of the efforts. A goal statement, when written properly, is the opposing *mirror* of the issue statement. It should address the issues on a broad scale. Goal statements are not quantifiable, whereas objectives are defined and measureable.

The goal statement is created by breaking down a few key factors and finessing the phrasing to match the *opposite* pieces of the issue statement in a way that is clear, defined, directed and connected to the target audience.

Example of a broken-down goal statement:

The goal of the _____ (client) is to _____ (goal—i.e., awareness, information, understanding, activation) by the target audience of _____ (target audience) on the subjects of _____, _____, _____ and _____ (focus of the goal).

The goal of the DJ Irie Foundation is the creation of an awareness campaign generating understanding throughout the youth of Miami-Dade County and their parents or caregivers of the music, dance and creative arts programs offered after school and through contest and events via traditional communication channels, social media and direct modes of communication.

Writing Objective Statements

Within a PR campaign, there is one issue statement and one goal statement, but there are many objectives that a campaign can aim to meet. These are measureable and easy to evaluate and to demonstrate if the campaign is effective and on the path toward success.

Objectives are usually defined by time or focus. Depending on the overall timeframe of the campaign, objectives can be either short term or long term. **Short-term objectives** fall within the timeline dictated by the execution schedule of the campaign. These are objectives that are completed within this calendar. **Long-term objectives** often start during the campaign, but have elements that are meant to be deployed after the campaign itself has ended. These are not measureable in relationship to the campaign alone.

Objectives are also defined by focus, such as informational, motivational, statutory, or financial. **Informational objectives** focus on what the audience needs to know or learn and are evaluated by how much knowledge was gained. **Motivational objectives** focus on the message the audience must retain and the motivation to act (buy, vote, write, etc.). **Statutory objectives** focus on policy decisions of government bodies and are usually associated with persuading voters and lobbying. **Financial objectives** are closely aligned with the outcomes of traditional marketing and are often used in integrated campaigns for products and services, which focus on sales or outcomes that are evaluated by financial gains (See Appendix Pages 175–176).

Writing objectives is often formulaic to eliminate confusion by the client and/or company. It is best to use the following model:

- Start with an action verb (*example: increase*)

- Insert measureable focus (*example: Facebook interactivity*)

- Input quantifiable number, a percentage is always best (*example: 20%*)

- Provide timeframe (*example: January–June*)

Example: Increase Facebook interactivity by 20% from January–June 2021

Theories

There are a number of theories that people employ when creating a Public Relations campaign. The more that the student understands the most commonly used theories, the more that they are able to create a viable campaign that is realistic with objectives that are on target, plausible and based on a foundation supported by research.

The most commonly used theories in Public Relations campaigns are

- Cognitive Dissonance Theory: Two contradictory beliefs or attitudes, as in you can believe in the platform of a person, but not like the actual person.

- Communication Accommodation Theory: Changing verbal and nonverbal styles to suit others, usually done through two ways: divergence and convergence.

- Confirmation Bias: Viewing the world in a light that reinforces his/her/their existing beliefs.

- Cultural Studies: Popular cultural is guided by the dominant class in society.

- Groupthink: Groups fail to critically analyze their options and maintain the group unity.

- Theory of Reasoned Action (TRA): Examines how behaviors are influenced by a person's intentions.

Communication theories are the basis of Public Relations campaigns. The more a practitioner understands the theories that are at the root of all mass communication plans, then they can create strategies and tactics to successfully address the objectives.

Theories in Application

Cognitive Dissonance Theory can be applied in PR Campaigns when it is clear that an audience is unwilling to *hear* opposing viewpoints. This occurs when people avoid hearing opposing viewpoints or change their beliefs to match their actions to reduce dissonance because they search for balance in their beliefs. The way to achieve success is to guide these groups toward balance.

Communication Accommodation Theory can be applied in PR Campaigns knowing that audiences adjust their communication styles to others. Depending on the audience, some opt to lean into the divergence method in which they highlight differences. The other audiences opt to lean toward the convergence method seeking social approval and focus on matching and mimicking communication styles to achieve acceptance.

Confirmation Bias is often used in PR Campaigns when an audience is difficult to reach because they have been identified as those who only select information and media that reinforce their existing ideas and beliefs. These audiences need more attention and specific tactics to persuade them to be open to new ideas.

Cultural Studies are used in PR Campaigns when people integrated elements of the mass media, which is often guided by profit and influenced by corporate ownership as opposed to knowledge seekers. This means that limiting the impact of existing media on a campaign could influence the outcome.

Groupthink is used in PR Campaigns when audiences are clearly thinking and acting as a group without critical analysis of the topic and individual application of knowledge and weighing alternatives. This is especially important for practitioners to understand as some audiences are predisposed to Groupthink.

Theory of Reasoned Action is often used in PR Campaigns when practitioners consider how to tap into messaging that influences behaviors that trigger attitudinal judgements or actions and social-normative considerations.

Messages and Themes

Often messages and themes are created after the situation analysis, audience analysis and research stages within a campaign are completed. Messages, created from written words or phrases, are much like slogans or tag lines used in advertising and marketing. This incorporates the *key message* that is the one phrase designed to be associated with the project. It is memorable to the target audience and is something of meaning to this group. Messages in general that are used throughout the campaign are carefully selected to match with the audience(s) and the outcomes.

Themes are usually more visual in nature and are heavily tested with the audience. Utilizing tools, such as a Visual Magnetism Index, graphic designers are able to match the color, content, imagery, typography and placement of thematic work to create memorable pieces that connect the audience with the campaign.

WORKSHEET 3A

WRITING THE ISSUE AND GOAL STATEMENTS

For this worksheet, you are to work with your group to write the issue, goal and objective for your campaign.

Part I: An ISSUE STATEMENT explains the challenges that the goal is to overcome, solve, resolve and so on. It is ONE sentence. It does not give background about WHY this is an issue, it is only the basics.

You answer this question to write the issue statement: What is the ONE problem we are trying to resolve?

DO ANY OF THE BELOW WORK AS AN ISSUE STATEMENT?

1. DJ Irie Foundation is unknown.

2. DJ Irie Foundation is a nonprofit unknown throughout the community because of lack of public awareness and interest in the subject.

Write a better one:

DJ Irie Foundation has limited
public awareness and community
involvement.

Part II: A GOAL is the ultimate condition of your having executed your campaign. It is ONE sentence. It does not explain how you will achieve it.

You answer this question to write the goal: What do you want the ultimate condition to be as the result of a successful campaign?

DO ANY OF THE BELOW WORK AS A GOAL?

1. For DJ Irie Foundation to gain regional recognition and volunteer support.

2. For DJ Irie Foundation to be well known.

Write a better one:

_____

_____

_____

_____

_____

_____

_____

_____

Part III: An OBJECTIVE tells what actions must be taken to achieve the plan's goal. Like a goal, it does not explain how you will achieve it, but it does indicate how you might measure and/or evaluate it.

It has three basic parts: (1) what the action is, (2) with whom the action is taken and (3) why the action is needed. It is specific and can be measured.

Now it's your turn to write some of your own. It is good practice to write examples for each of the various types:

Short-term objective example:

_____

_____

_____

_____

Long-term objective example:

_____

_____

_____

_____

_____

Informational objective example:

_____

_____

_____

_____

Motivational objective example:

_____

_____

_____

_____

Statutory objective example:

_____

_____

_____

_____

_____

Financial objective example:

_____

_____

_____

_____

_____

WORKSHEET 3B

APPLICATION OF THEORIES

For this worksheet, you and your team must determine what theory is most likely used within this PR campaign. Note that your team is not limited to those listed within the chapter, but your team must *support* your determination.

What are the possible theories used?

_____

_____

_____

_____

_____

_____

_____

_____

What theory do you think is used?

_____

_____

_____

_____

_____

_____

_____

_____

_____

What explanation would you give to the client to support your determination? How would you explain that this theory is used within the PR Campaign?

_____

_____

_____

_____

_____

_____

_____

_____

_____

CHAPTER 4

DEFINING THE TARGET AUDIENCE

WHO IS YOUR AUDIENCE?

What Are the Demographics?

Before your team can begin to define the target audience, it's extremely important to understand the basic population and particular groups within that popular, which is the most basic definition of demographics. Within the fields of marketing, Public Relations and even on larger scales of data collection such as the Census Bureau and U.S. Department of Labor, the term *demographics* often refers to characteristics about individuals such as age, gender and ethnicity, which the individuals have little-to-no control over, yet are ways that these individuals are grouped together.

Gender

A study released in April 2018 by the U.S. Bureau of Labor Statistics titled "Assessing the Feasibility of Asking about Gender Identity in Current Population Survey . . ." explained the options of ways to ask about gender identity. Options include: male, female, transgender, genderqueer and other (specify). A possible additional option is to offer options for the transgender choice including: transgender-male to female; transgender-female to male; or transgender-gender nonconforming.

Ethnicity

Most companies opt to follow a standard base for choices of race. This is not asking for people to identify their ethnic origins (as in DNA tests, etc.). Most companies use breakdowns to identify their target audience that are similar to those used by the Census Bureau of U.S. Bureau of Labor Statistics. The Census offers the following options: White (non-Hispanic), Black (non-Hispanic), Asian (non-Hispanic), Native-American (non-Hispanic), Hispanic and other. The Bureau of Labor Statistics offers the following options: American Indians and Alaska Natives, Asian, Black or African American, Hispanic or Latino, Native Hawaiian or Pacific Islander, Mixed Race, White and other.

Age

There are a number of general similarities that member of specific generations share because of factors that influence people as they progress through school and life, such as technology, politics, events (celebrations, natural disasters, acts of terrorism, etc.), economic standards, social movements and more. Most marketing and Public Relations practitioners use the following years and divisions for generational groups:

- The Greatest Generation (1901–1926)

- The Silent Generation (1927–1946)

- Baby Boomers Generation (1946–1964)

- Generation X (1965–1980)

- Xennials, A Gap Generation Between Gen X and Gen Y (1977–1983)

- Generation Y, Millennials (1981–2000)

- Centennials, A Gap Generation Between Gen Y and Gen Z (1995–2008)

- Generation Z, i Generation (2001–now)

What Are the Psychographics?

After the team has narrowed down some of the larger areas of focus including gender, ethnicity and age, the focus can shift to psychographics. Psychographics are characteristics that individuals can control such as education, family size, income, marital status, religion and so on. All these may or may not be relevant to the campaign.

The best way to incorporate psychographics is to determine what characteristics are necessary to know to include the largest possible target audience. For example, is religious preferences something that is relevant for a nonprofit creating a campaign focusing on education options for children. Perhaps not, but does education level of the audience matter, perhaps.

Psychographic groupings are often very useful in defining an audience. Using Education Level or Income Level for a specific target audience or a secondary audience can sometimes determine highly directed tactical pieces that yield action or response and often lead to the success of a PR campaign. Again, people are the root of the PR campaign, which should never be overlooked. Therefore, if having an income of more than $100,000 per year or having at least a bachelor's degree is useful knowledge and can create a more strategic tactical strike, then it is worth it to delve into an explanation of what type of person fits those criteria.

Specialty Audiences

Often lumped into other groups, there are a few groups that cross into other already-defined audiences, but are a specialty in their collective power. Religious groups, political groups, LGBTQ+ groups and disabled groups are examples of such specialty audiences.

Often these groups have members who identify as different genders and ethnicities and are different ages, but collectively, they have a unifying voice and a power behind their ability to harness or leverage the people within specialty audiences.

The LGBTQ+ community is often misunderstood or characterized with derogatory assumptions. Many school and workplaces that are progressive have adopted the use of asking for gender pronouns, this allows the individual to self-identify as male, female, or other using the pronouns he, she, or they. Some workplaces have changed to share-able gender inclusive bathrooms that are, in essence, unisex. The collective voice asking for more understanding, education and acceptance has led to some revisions of workplace policies, but it is their lobbying and buying power that yields them the best results regarding getting businesses and organizations to listen.

Religious groups have had moments throughout history of yielding great power and influence and moments when the public attention and scrutiny has forced people within these groups to hide their beliefs in public forums. The volume of practicing religious believers is what makes these groups so strong in the larger marketplace and groups that are impossible to ignore.

The disabled community has fought for more than 50 years for their right to be acknowledged, heard and recognized for their contributions and their attributes. The community of people is not always the largest or the most vocal, but they have been strategic in their visibility, their alliances and their efforts to impact the larger culture. Removal of the *R* word from common spoken vernacular was a big step that so many within the disabled community took up as their own personal cause.

Political parties yield a lot of power within the American democratic system, but it is more than just self-identifying as a conservative or liberal. This group has the power to create and enforce law, bestow accolades and shame those for perpetuating falsehoods.

Each of these above examples and the myriad of other specialty audiences can all impact how a PR campaign is created and executed and the final results. Most specialty audiences can shine a light and help spread the word through their own means and among their own members efficiently and with finesse.

Painting a Picture of the Audience

To paint an accurate picture of *who* is the audience for the project, it is best to begin by accurately describing the generations, ethnicities and genders. If a project works for all genders, then that allows for more flexibility in messaging. However, to create key messages appropriate for your target audience, it's important that the description of the audience be clear. If the range of ages of the possible audience members is from Baby Boomers through Millennials, then it is possible to start with the oldest generation and work to the youngest through an accurate description (See Appendix Page 154–158).

Pre-Packaged Audiences

When a team begins to *paint the picture* of who is the audience, the prepackaged audience is a group of people who have been grouped together for a reason that pre-dated the project. These pre-packaged audiences have agreed to join together, usually voluntarily, because of common interests or shared beliefs. Some examples of these groups are professional organizations (American Marketing Association, National Association of Sales Professionals, Public Relations Society of America), groups with shared interests (National Audubon Society, National Rifle Association, People for the Ethical Treatment of Animals, Sierra Club), groups based on geography (Northeast Leadership Council, South Bay Neighborhood), or groups based on other psychographic characteristics such as religion or education (Coastal Christian Alliance, State College Alumni Association).

When creating a full picture of the target audience, use several prepackaged audiences to create a complete 360-degree picture. Start by writing one or two sentences about why this prepackaged audience fits into the audience scope and ends with basic analysis of membership basics.

Opinion Leaders

Within Public Relations, opinion leaders are divided into two categories (formal and informal). Formal opinion leaders are people who are voted into public office (elected officials such as a City Commissioner, Mayor, or Governor) and in some cases people elected into positions to offer guidance and/or authority (school board members, judges). Informal opinion leaders are those who are elected either by public opinion (meaning celebrities, athletes, reality television stars and social media influencers) or those elected by their peers because they are considered to be an authority on a subject (such as a president of a school group, leader of a women's group).

When writing this into the description of your target audience, you should consider making a list of your opinion leaders from both groups. Additionally, the team should make a wish list that includes those individuals who are your desired people. This list should have double the amount of people on it than the team actually wishes to use because some people may not agree to be included in the group. The idea is that you begin to request participation from the people who are high on your wish list and work from that point.

> *Note:* The single most common mistake I see in creating a target audience analysis is at the stage when students must identify appropriate prepackaged audiences and opinion leaders. I often give my classes the rule of thumb that you must be able to **communicate directly** with the people within this group. So it's not appropriate to say for Generation Z that all the students within a school district are a prepackaged audience because most school districts are not going to permit outside organizations to have lists of their students or give their students messaging from a third party. The better approach is to consider other ways to reach the same students such as through clubs and organizations, religious groups, volunteer organizations, or even social media groups. Please understand that a social media channel alone is not enough of a direct communication method, but a Facebook group for example would be a perfect channel of directed communication.

WORKSHEET 4A

TARGET AUDIENCE

DEMOGRAPHICS

Which gender/s are most appropriate for this project? Male, female, transgender?

all genders

_____

_____

_____

_____

Which ethnicities are most appropriate for this project?

- American Indians and Alaska Natives: _____
- Asian: _____
- Black or African American: _____
- Hispanic or Latino: _____
- Native Hawaiian or Pacific Islander: _____
- Mixed Race: _____
- White: _____
- Other: _____

Which ethnicities are local to the region or area?

_____

_____

_____

_____

_____

Which age group/s are the most appropriate for this project?

- The Greatest Generation (1901–1926): _____
- The Silent Generation (1927–1946): _____

- Baby Boomers Generation (1946–1964): _____

- Generation X (1965–1980): _____

- Xennials, A Gap Generation Between Gen X and Gen Y (1977–1983): _____
  _____

- Generation Y, Millennials (1981–2000): _____

- Centennials, A Gap Generation Between Gen Y and Gen Z (1995–2008): _____
  _____

- Generation Z, i Generation (2001–now): _____

Which generations are the best audience for the messaging and have the highest likelihood of activating?

_____

_____

_____

_____

_____

PSYCHOGRAPHICS

What other forms of *grouping* are helpful to paint the picture of the audience for whom the team is creating messaging to reach? Which of the following are possible psychographics that the campaign might focus on reaching?

- Education (highest level completed):
  - General Education Degree (GED)
  - High School Diploma
  - Associate's Degree
  - Technical Degree
  - Bachelor's Degree
  - Master's Degree (MBA, MFA, etc.)
  - Medical Doctorate (DO, DVM, MD, DS, etc.)
  - Doctorate (PhD, EdD, JD, etc.)

- Religion:
  - Christian
  - Islam
  - Judaism
  - Mormon

- o Protestant
  - o Other: _____

- Marital Status:
  - o Single
  - o Married
  - o Divorced
  - o Widowed
  - o Legally Separated
  - o Other: _____

- Income (Per Household):
  - o Number of people within the household that earn an annual income: 1, 2, 3, 4, 5+
  - o Income Level:
    - $250,000+
    - $150,000–249,999
    - $100,000–149,999
    - $75,000–99,999
    - $50,000–74,999
    - $30,000–9,999
    - $15,500–29,999

Which psychographic groups are the most useful to create a full dossier on the target audience?

_____

_____

_____

_____

_____

_____

_____

_____

_____

PREPACKED AUDIENCES AND OPINION LEADERS

What types of prepackaged groups can be used as prepackaged audiences?

_____

_____

_____

_____

_____

_____

_____

_____

_____

Who might be a valuable opinion leader to reach the various generational groups and why?

_____

_____

_____

_____

_____

_____

_____

_____

WRITING THE DESCRIPTION

Knowing what the team has learned about the target audience, what *summations* can you make about the messaging and best ways to reach the audience? How does the team use social media? How does the team use traditional media?

_____

_____

_____

_____

_____

_____

_____

_____

CHAPTER 5

CREATING A RESEARCH PLAN

EVERYTHING STARTS WITH A PLAN

A research plan can have a few different sections, which usually just depends on the PR campaign and the needs of the project and the client. In some cases, the client provides a large amount of data or gives access to its databases. This provides a wonderful resource of information.

The plan for all research is to learn what has already been done by researchers and information from other industry-specific articles. After this research is collected, a primary research plan is created to develop a tool and deploy a study to learn specific knowledge that answers key questions relevant to the PR campaign. This primary research results in original conclusions, which can be directly applied to the PR campaign.

Research is the starting point to all unanswered questions beyond the basic depiction of the target audience. This is important because it drives the decision-making process and leads to a stronger PR campaign for the client.

Examination of Gifted Data

Client data are just that, information provided by the client. On occasion a client offers up the raw data from a recent survey or focus group. This information might be exactly what is needed. Although the data is *free* in the sense that it does not take any time or effort to collect, it might not be worded correctly or it might be too *self-serving* in nature.

No matter what is needed for the project, any information provided by the source should be used in some way or another. Using the study data to answer critical questions when possible is great. If that is not possible, then deduce what results are similar to questions that pertain to the PR campaign and create some basic connections.

It is not in the best interest of the PR campaign to write in these connections as facts but hypothesis that are later supported by original primary research. Most clients want to know that their own research is valid and also want to feel that the PR campaign they are paying for has original research to answer necessary questions.

Secondary Research Plan

The secondary research plan begins with a review of topics needed for examination. The topics examined in secondary research should be both focused and comprehensive. Not every topic listed is appropriate for examination using secondary research. This requires using research search engines such as Lexis Nexis, iSeek, RefSeek or links provided by the school library.

The topics for Secondary Research are what can make the entire review of existing data and conclusions. This provides the basis for the primary research study. Each study used contributes to the knowledge gained. Conclusions can be drawn per topic or per section. Each topic of study offers insights to work and previous studies completed and areas of research not yet examined.

Primary Research Plan

The primary research plan begins with creating a list of what information is still needed after the full secondary research study is completed. Whatever knowledge that is missing should be included in the primary research and the type of tool used should be determined by what access the class or team has to research subjects and time to execute the research plan.

The team must choose between qualitative and quantitative research. Does the client have access to a volume of people with the target audience, or does the team have access to this pool of research candidates? If so, then quantitative research might be a wonderful option as it allows the researchers to include a variety of topics in one survey. If the survey can be administered online or in-person to semi-captive audience, then it's something that can often yield really useful insights. If the pool of research candidates is small, then the consideration should be to use a qualitative research option. These research tools include focus groups and interviews. There are other research tool options.

Primary research must include demographics so the research team can create correlations that are meaningful and specific to the PR campaign.

> *Example:* Of the Millennials who responded yes to the usage of social media *daily* to seek information on events, 47% also engaged with the event by posting, checking in, or tagging the organization in photos.

Dividing Responsibilities

Each person on the team should be responsible for contributing to the overall secondary research and primary research for the PR campaign. It allows for a well-rounded and full-bodied secondary research summary if each person examines one to three topics. Each topic should have a minimum of five articles incorporated into the review. A five-person team then has at least 15 topics covered utilizing approximately 60 to 75 articles.

Additionally, each person in the team is responsible for participating in the primary research data collection. Once the minimum collection number is established, each student in the course should have a data collection plan that includes a date, time and location for data location, plus a minimum number of subjects. Primary research only works if the pool is representative, so it is important that the data collection is done in locations that are relevant to the project.

Finally, inputting the data should also be a shared responsibility. This can be spearheaded by the group of students leading the research division. Enter the data into programs such as SPSS Statistics, Tableau, Statgraphics and many more. Two-person teams to input the data makes the work quicker and more efficient. Human error during data entry is reduced if there is a partner system with a check-and-review at the end.

WORKSHEET 5A

CHECKLIST FOR RESEARCH PLAN

Does the team have any of the following?

_____ Client Data

_____ Previous Study Data

_____ Previous Campaign Research

Has the team designed a secondary research plan?

Person 1:

Topic _____ Topic _____

Topic _____ Topic _____

Person 2:

Topic _____ Topic _____

Topic _____ Topic _____

Person 3:

Topic _____ Topic _____

Topic _____ Topic _____

Person 4:

Topic _____ Topic _____

Topic _____ Topic _____

Person 5:

Topic _____ Topic _____

Topic _____ Topic _____

Person 6:

Topic _____ Topic _____

Topic _____ Topic _____

What tools is the team considering for primary research?

_____ Quantitative Research: Survey

_____ Qualitative Research: Focus Group

_____ Qualitative Research: Interview

CHAPTER 6

RESEARCH FOR THE CLIENT

STARTING WITH SECONDARY RESEARCH

Secondary research is the foundation and starting point for all PR campaigns. As the team is creating the situation analysis and SWOT and working to paint an accurate picture of the target audience, the team can also begin to begin their research.

Secondary research is similar to a literature review in academic papers. This is the collection of previously completed research studies that have conclusions or results that are related to topics within the PR campaign. Secondary research summaries begin with an introduction to the topics, summaries by topic and conclusions.

Comprehensive secondary research summaries must have a diverse array of topics that have a direct connection to the campaign topics. The secondary research summary often has academic in-text citations to credit those who have completed the research that is used in the PR campaign. The secondary research summary must be complete with a full list of references in whatever research style is acceptable by both the client and the academic institution.

Acceptable forms of citation and referencing include:

- American Psychological Association (APA)

- Chicago Manual Style Guide

- MLA Style Manual

Referencing is critically important to the secondary reference summary as it allows for the client to see how the previous research is applied to resolve the issue. The secondary research summary is the basis for decisions made on how to approach the primary research. The approach to primary research is to determine what information is missing from the secondary research summary and examine the best way to gather that information using an effective tool.

Defining Topics

Creating a secondary research summary is only as strong as the topics covered. Often secondary research summaries are too short and/or shallow or too comprehensive and/or long. The best way to know if the summary covers all the topics needed is to ask after it has been complete if there is anything that has not been covered.

Example: In a PR campaign for a nonprofit aimed to provide after-school programming for children in urban areas. Research topics are children's programs, enriching programs for children, children in urban areas learning styles, social media engagement for families in urban areas, engagement for children-related initiatives, communication channels for parents to choose programs for their children and interest-based programming.

Subtopics for secondary research summaries are often grouped together into larger topic areas and then also have sub-subtopics to divvying up the areas of research even smaller. In the end, the research plan ends up looking like a tree with a branch and several smaller branches stemming off of the original. See Figure 6.1 to understand how this works and how to consider creating a research plan tree for the PR campaign the team is working on. It's important that there not be an ego or the thought that any topic area is too broad or sub-subtopic is too small. Sometimes the topic of defining terms seems like it is not needed, yet it is the most crucial piece of secondary research because it sets the groundwork for all research that follows and ensures that all parties are conversing about the same elements and using the same key terms.

The choice of what to cover in secondary research summaries is decided by the team of researchers. Not everything in Figure 6.1 might be useful as a research subtopic to examine. By creating a research plan (tree), the entire team can see the topics covered in each category before the research collection phase begins and make decisions based on if the topic is relevant to the PR campaign.

It is not always the most obvious choices that are the most effective for inclusion in a secondary research summary. Many times, the intuition is to search for "successful PR campaigns in children's programming" or something similar, but utilizing previous campaigns

Figure 6.1 Example of a Secondary Research Summary Plan Tree for a PR Campaign for a Nonprofit Aimed to Provide After-School Programming for Children in Urban Areas

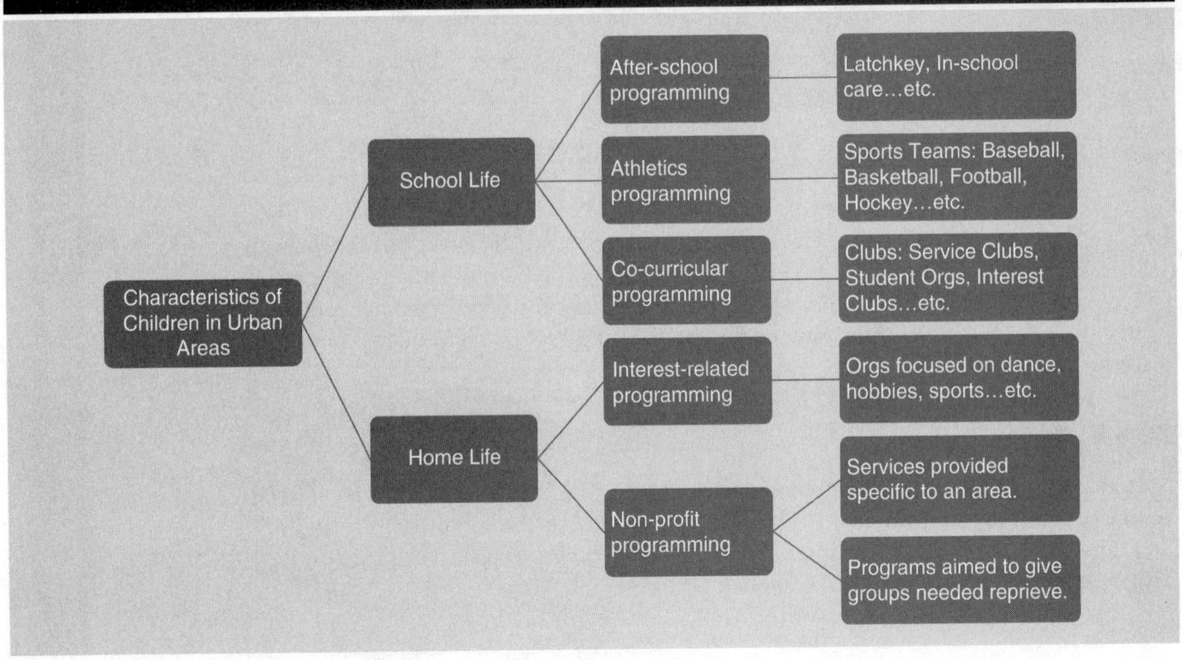

without any other research is too narrow of a focus. Research summaries should be scattered in multiple directions so that every possible avenue is covered. This creates a more comprehensive approach and leaves less for the primary research to cover.

Breaking Down the Summaries

There are a number of approaches to how to write a secondary research summary from a group standpoint. The way that creates the most cohesive final product is to ask each member of the team to tackle an entire topic, including all the subtopics and sub-subtopics that lie within the larger topic. This means that in the end, when one or two people from the team attempt to weave together all the writing, it is in larger chunks of information rather than in small pieces.

If each person on the team has at least one topic to write about then it means that he/she/they should be collecting a minimum of 5 to 7 articles to support each subtopic. More articles are better as this only leads to the depth and scope of the content. Each student can colorcode the content in each article by sub-subtopic using highlighters or do whatever system works best for him/her/them. When selecting articles, look for those that have multiple uses and can be used to touch on several topics in the subtopics or sub-subtopics.

Some of the articles collected may not be used in the final summary analysis. The final selection of articles used are those that have the most useful information for the summation of material.

Writing the Summary

The secondary research summary should be organized in the following format:

1. Introduction
    a. First Topic
        i. Subtopic
            1. Sub-subtopic
            2. Sub-subtopic
            3. Subtopic
        ii. Sub-subtopic
            1. Sub-subtopic
        iii. Subtopic
            1. Sub-subtopic 1
            2. Sub-subtopic
    b. Second Topic
        i. Subtopic
            1. Sub-subtopic 1
            2. Sub-subtopic
            3. Subtopic
        ii. Sub-subtopic
            1. Sub-subtopic
    c. Third Topic
        i. Subtopic
            1. Sub-subtopic
            2. Sub-subtopic
        ii. Subtopic
            1. Sub-subtopic
            2. Sub-subtopic

       iii. Subtopic
          1. Sub-subtopic
          2. Sub-subtopic

   2. Conclusions

This format is a classic literature review format. The benefit to writing in this format is that it demonstrates to the client that multiple sources support that topic or idea. A client often asks, "Can you explain more about how or why you made the decisions you did?"

If a client understands that there are a number of articles that support the topic, there is no need to ask the question of how or why. The answer is provided by the research. By *weaving* together the various articles that support the topic, this ensures the secondary research summary does not read like a book report.

As a class or team, the decision should be made in advance what type of research format is used and if in-text citations or footnotes are preferred by the client. Either offers the client understanding what pieces of the research summary were extrapolated from which articles.

At the end of each sub-subtopic it is best if there are conclusions or summations drawn. This makes it cleaner for the final conclusion paragraph in which there are overall conclusions drawn (See Appendix Pages 159–163)

Secondary Research Finale

There is not a minimum or maximum length for a comprehensive secondary research summary. Rather, when the teams through the summary, it should be obvious if it was thorough enough if afterward there are no remaining questions that are unanswered that are not clearly addressed with primary research.

For a simple topic, perhaps there are only a few topics with a tree that only branches three deep. For a complex topic, there might be as many as five to seven topics that extend four braches deep. Again, this is all subjective to what the project encompasses and how much can be found on the topics.

WORKSHEET 6A

CREATING A RESEARCH TOPIC TREE

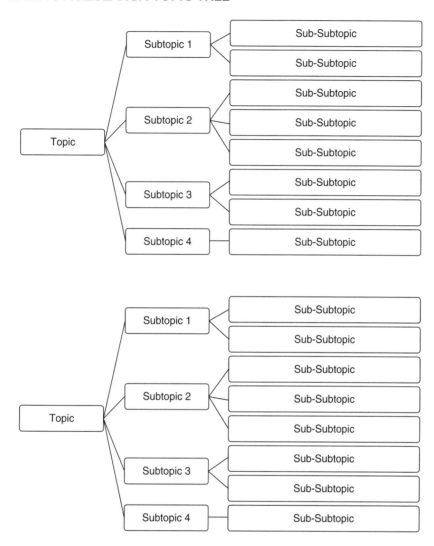

WORKSHEET 6B

ORGANIZING TOPICS AND ARTICLES

Topic:

_____

Subtopics and Sub-Subtopics:

_____

_____

Articles Related to Topic/Subtopic:

_____

_____

_____

_____

_____

Topic:

_____

Subtopics and Sub-Subtopics:

_____

_____

Articles Related to Topic/Subtopic:

_____

_____

_____

_____

_____

Topic:

_____

Subtopics and Sub-Subtopics:

_____

_____

Articles Related to Topic/Subtopic:

_____

_____

_____

_____

_____

Topic:

_____

Subtopics and Sub-Subtopics:

_____

_____

Articles Related to Topic/Subtopic:

_____

_____

_____

_____

Topic:

_____

Subtopics and Sub-Subtopics:

_____

_____

Articles Related to Topic/Subtopic:

_____

_____

_____

_____

_____

Topic:

_____

Subtopics and Sub-Subtopics:

_____

_____

Articles Related to Topic/Subtopic:

_____

_____

_____

_____

_____

Topic:

_____

Subtopics and Sub-Subtopics:

_____

_____

Articles Related to Topic/Subtopic:

_____

_____

_____

_____

_____

WORKSHEET 6C

ASSIGNING WRITING RESPONSIBILITIES AND NEXT STEPS

TOPIC: RESEARCHER:

_____   _____

_____   _____

_____   _____

_____   _____

_____   _____

_____   _____

What are the areas that the secondary research summary did not cover that are NEEDED for the PR campaign to move forward? Determine which of these topics are necessary on a scale of 1–3 (3 as essential) and then score the topics after adding the scores of everyone on the team together.

TOPIC MISSING: NECESSITY SCORE (1-low, 2-useful, 3-essential):

_____   _____

_____   _____

_____   _____

_____   _____

_____   _____

_____   _____

_____   _____

_____   _____

_____   _____

CHAPTER 7

PRIMARY RESEARCH FOR THE CLIENT

DETERMINING THE TOOL AND THE INFORMATION TO GATHER

The secondary research summary explores in-depth the topics that are determined to be the most important to the PR campaign in terms of foundational information. This also spotlights the gaps in knowledge where there is not enough information on specific subjects or where the information is not focused enough on a topic closely related to the focus of the PR campaign. For example, there might be research about programming for youth, but it might not have specifics about the programming in urban versus rural areas.

The gaps in information provide a road map that can be considered as the basis for what are the primary research and the research conclusions that the PR campaign is based on. The primary research segment of a PR campaign includes the steps of planning, implementation, data collection, interpretation and conclusions. These steps are not uncommon in research or in campaigns, but are essential to building a proper campaign, backed by both secondary and primary research.

Finding the Right Tool for the Research

Data collection can be successful or unsuccessful based on the tool used. The best place to begin is to take the gaps in knowledge from the secondary research summary and determine which of these unanswered topics are most important to include in the overall research findings.

Once these knowledge gaps have been determined, then it is important to ask two questions:

- What is the best way to ask questions that yield information from where we can extrapolate and draw conclusions?

- What types of people are in the predetermined target audience group and, of these, how many are likely to answer and respond when they are usually not the most effective.

Once the right tool has been determined, then the researchers have to write the questions, beta test the tool and eventually deploy the instrument. Although there are some basic rules to follow to create the best possible tool, there is not a one-size-fits-all policy to the tools.

Creating Primary Research, Using Research Tools

Quantitative Research

If the client has access to a pool of candidates that can be used as subjects for research purposes or a pool of people who are within the target audience range, then quantitative research may be the best choice.

Choosing quantitative research means you have access to the following:

- Pool of research candidates who fit within the target audience demographics. The pool must be at least a minimum of 500 to 1,000 people.

- Ability to deliver the research tool to the people who are eligible via email or social media.

The most common quantitative research tool is a questionnaire. The survey begins with demographics data information such as

- Age
- Ethnicity
- Gender

And psychographic data information such as

- Education
- Geographic Region
- Income
- Religion

The rest of the questionnaire is broken into groups of needed information. This should be organized in a way that is logical. Most questionnaires are no more than 10 minutes maximum to complete and the number of questions varies based on the format the questions used.

Question formats used most common are

- Yes/No
- Likert Scale (Strongly Agree, Agree, Undecided, Disagree, Strongly Disagree)
- Scale/Order (Best to Worst)
- Hot Zone (Region or Zone)

If the person answering the questions must have certain *qualities* to be part of the research, then qualifying questions are best to use. The questions are fast and easy to answer. The response of "No" usually means the survey taker skips to a later question because he/she/they do not qualify to continue.

Gathering Data From Quantitative Research

Once the questionnaire is created, the tool must be beta tested with a group of people who fit within the target audience, but may be qualify as research subjects. These are often people who are too close to the researchers such as friends, family, roommates and so on. These beta testers are asked to take the survey and look for grammatical errors, comprehension issues, or glitches in the technology.

BETA testing is done before the tool is deployed and any issues the beta testers identify must be revised or edited. The final tool is ready for deployment when the edits are completed.

After deployment, quantitative research requires a high volume of people to participate. The greater the number, the more accurate the responses are of the general target audience. Research should be administered for an extended period of time so that he/she/they can take the survey at a time that works best.

Once the responses are completed, the data should be transferred into a statistics system such as SPSS data analysis software or something similar. These software systems allow the researcher to input any specifics and include the replies to each question.

After the data is input, then basic conclusions can be drawn. This analysis is information such as 68% of those who responded stated that they use social media to determine what events they attend each weekend. After these basic conclusions are drawn, then more complex correlations can be drawn between specific questions and the reply plus specific demographic groups.

Example: Of the 68% of those who responded that they use social media to determine what events to attend each weekend, 52% are women who are the decision makers in their home.

Conclusions are very important to the big picture, but it's the correlations that are ultimately extremely important to the final PR campaign. The specific connections between the questions asked and the subsets of the people within the target audience can answer a lot of questions and create a strong plan for success that drives the creation of tactical elements for the PR campaign.

Qualitative Research

If the client doesn't have access to a large candidate pool or no candidate pool at all or if the questions that need to be answered are more long format, then it might be best to consider qualitative research. This research is best if the client needs to know more of the behavioral and emotional reasons as part of the decision making, not just simply did you do this, yes or no, but why and for what reasons.

Choosing qualitative research means the researchers must have:

- Questions that are more in-depth

- Access to interview spaces or private areas

- The most common qualitative research tool is a focus group and in-person interviews.

The focus group/interview begins with demographics data (usually written) information such as

- Age

- Ethnicity

- Gender

- And more

And psychographic data information such as

- Education
- Geographic Region
- Income
- Religion

Gathering Data From Quantitative Research

The questions are grouped together by like topics so that there is an easy transition. Most focus groups and Interviews are 15 to 30 minutes in length. There are a few tips to ensure that all research is properly administered.

Focus Group Tips:

- Proctor plus 5 to 7 subjects
- Subjects should be a range of the people within the target audience.
- Each subject should speak at least two times, so the proctor must *control* the room.
- Questions should be asked in a pyramid format starting from more important to least important.
- Focus groups should be a maximum of 30 to 40 minutes.
- Focus groups should be video recorded.
- A transcript should be created following the focus group.

In-person interview tips:

- Subjects used in the study should be a range of the target audience requirements.
- Interview should be a maximum of 30 minutes.
- Interviews should be video and/or audio recorded.
- Interviewer should have follow-up questions for the questions that are key to the study.
- A transcript should be created following the interview.

The questions should be beta tested before the focus group or interview should be administered. This beta test can be done with similar people to the target audience, but does not have to done in an interview or focus group format.

The downside to focus groups:

- Proctor must be able to *control* the room.
- Strong personalities can hijack the conversation.
- People can get off track and the topics can be misconstrued.
- Too many people or too few people can change the dynamic of the conversation.

- Transcripts are hard to follow.

- At least three to five focus groups must be completed for the information to useful.

The downside to in-person interviews:

- Interviewee can be too conversational or too friendly.

- People can get off track and the topics can be misconstrued.

- Transcripts are hard to follow.

- The types of people interviewed must be within the target audience and must not be connected to the Interviewee.

Conclusions drawn from qualitative research are not based as much on overall percentages as much as it is from the information gathered. Specific terms or statements made are impactful for the client and useful for the PR campaign. The results and conclusions are specific to the questions asked and are often written in collective statements such as 92% of those who participated answered that they plan far in advance when attending events and one commented that she publically confirms attending events online through social media for charity and other such events that are those who she wants to maintain her connection to or have others follow her example and donate. Specifically worded examples such as this are very useful for a PR campaign as this is how the tactical elements are created and critical decisions are made.

Playing the Odds

Regardless of if the team opts to use quantitative or qualitative research, there is a minimum number of people in which the team must have as subjects. The best numbers to use are a minimum of 500 for surveys/questionnaires. Again, the higher the volume, the more accurate the information is as a representative model of what the overall target audience is thinking or feeling. For qualitative research, it is best to have an odd number of focus groups (three to five with at least five to seven members of each focus group). This means that for focus groups, there is a range of 15 to 35 participants that represent a much larger audience. In-person interviews should be the same range of 20 to 40 interviews.

The best way to conduct research is for every person in the class or on the team to participate in data collection. This means that if the researchers opt to go with a quantitative research method, then deployment of the tool to subjects is on the entire team or class. Each person should have a list of people that he/she/they can administer the survey to as well as those names offered by the client.

Additionally, for the qualitative research, the best focus groups have only one person who is the proctor for all of the groups. The researchers have to maintain consistency for all focus groups and interviews. The focus groups should have researchers watching live and taking notes about the nonverbal interactions. The in-person interviews should be practiced in advance so that each person administering the interviews read the questions the same and offer the same follow-up questions.

Even after trying to get the proper numbers and maintaining consistency, there is always the chance that some of the interviews have to be tossed out because they are not valid. Every time research is conducted, it is a gamble in which the researchers are playing the odds, just making sure they at least get the minimum.

Writing Research Results

Delivering research results to the client, it is best to provide a mix of written results, infographics and data-driven charts. These combinations are the best way for the client to comprehend the results of the research.

The results of the research should be delivered with a summation of the total numbers and demographics first. The numbers and demographics breakdown is key to demonstrating that the target audience is represented.

The next few sections of the research begin with the basic conclusions. This should be a mix of the charts, infographics and written explanations. This is not question-by-question, but rather an overall of the most important data collected. The information delivered should be what is most impactful to the PR campaign. This is often 7 to 10 pieces of key information.

The next set of results delivered is often correlations. These are easier if delivered as complex infographics with a written explanation in the breakdown (See Appendix Pages 164–172).

Figure 7.1   Infographic for the 50% of Women Who Responded "Yes" to Using Social Media for Planning to Attend Events, Broken Down by Generation

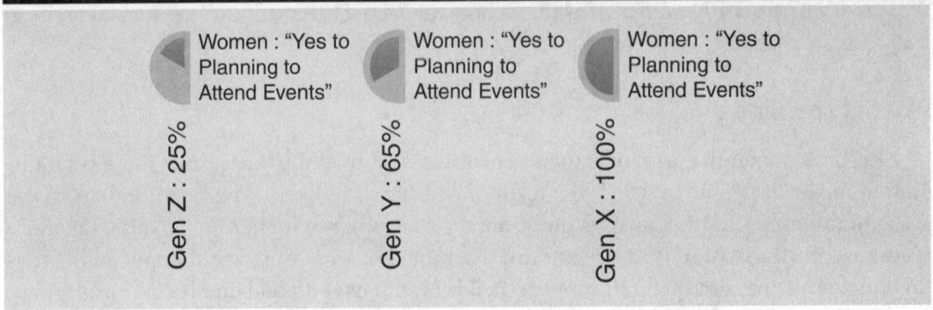

WORKSHEET 7A

PICKING YOUR QUESTIONS

Part I: Pulling questions from secondary research summary.

What are the gaps that have been identified that were not answered in the secondary research summary?

_____

_____

_____

_____

_____

Part II: What does the research dictate is the best tool to use?

_____ Pool of research candidates

_____ Few research candidates

_____ Research questions for quantitative data

_____ Open-ended research questions for qualitative data

WORKSHEET 7B

BRAINSTORMING QUESTIONS

Part I: Demographics Questions

_____ Age   _____   _____

_____ Ethnicity   _____   _____

_____ Gender   _____   _____

Part II: Psychographics Questions

_____ Education   _____   _____

_____ Geographical region   _____   _____

_____ Income   _____   _____

_____ Religion   _____   _____

Part III: Group Topics for Questions

Group 1: _____

Sample Questions:

_____

_____

_____

_____

_____

_____

Group 2: _____

Sample Questions:

_____

_____

_____

_____

_____

_____

Group 3: _____

Sample Questions:

_____

_____

_____

_____

_____

_____

Group 4: _____

Sample Questions:

_____

_____

_____

_____

_____

_____

Group 5: _____

Sample Questions:

_____

_____

_____

_____

_____

_____

WORKSHEET 7C

IDENTIFICATION OF SUBJECTS AND BETA TESTERS

Beta Testers:

There should be at least 5 to 10 beta testers who can review the tool. If each person identifies a person who is disqualified as a research subject, but is perfect to be a beta tester, this is the most efficient way to find beta testers.

Create a list of those people who are beta testers. Put them listed by their name, what category the person is in and then who in the class or team is related to the beta tester and why the person is disqualified.

NAME: CATEGORY/DEMOGRAPHICS: PERSON/DISQUALIFIED:

_____

_____

_____

_____

_____

_____

_____

_____

_____

_____

_____

_____

_____

_____

_____

WORKSHEET 7D

DRAWING SOME CHARTS AND INFOGRAPHIC IDEAS

Select five pieces of key data that you believe should be turned into a chart of infographic. Using the boxes below, draw out the information to determine what is the best way to visually present this material to the client. Most time, if you dummy this content first, the final outcome is better than if you use Canva or a preset design aid and use something that has been pre-created and is not as unique to the client.

Data:

_____

_____

_____

_____

_____

Data:

_____

_____

Data:

CHAPTER 8

OUTLINING YOUR SITUATION ANALYSIS

SITUATION ANALYSIS FIRST

Starting With Assessing the Client

Proper assessment of the company and/or client begins with looking closely at the situation from a 360 degree viewpoint. Most companies and clients are not always honest with themselves or the depiction of their current situation. Therefore, it is vital that when writing a situation analysis and SWOT, each person is objective in his/her/their assessments.

The following outlines the different sections that must be included in the four sections of a situation analysis and SWOT and the best way to write this for a company and/or client that is easiest for comprehension and execution.

The situation analysis is *broader* than just what is placed into a SWOT analysis. For the client, each student in the class should individually write their own situation analysis (in paragraph form, using proper subheads), which includes summaries on client background, internal audit or assessment, public perception and external audit or assessment. The SWOT is best delivered in bullet form using complete sentences with action verbs. If each person on a team writes their own SWOT, then the final client plan would include the best pieces from the team/s.

Situation Analysis

There are a few tips when writing the situation analysis for the company or client. Be careful to write in a neutral voice without bias. This approach will give the company or client hope that the campaign has the ability to resolve the issue and offer successful tactics to meet the objectives. Each section of the situation analysis is written with brevity and clarity in mind. Each section should be a maximum of one page (See Appendix Pages 147–151).

Client Background is a brief introduction to the client. This is factual and is not subjective or biased in any way. Think of this as the About Us page on a company website, although you do not want to use that heading. This is something that is created specifically for the client and includes facts such as history, important figures, growth of the company, specializations, or anything that is relevant to the issue and goal of the campaign.

Internal Audit or Assessment is a description of what the company or client has done thus far. This is internal to the company and includes what the company has in existence, what changes have been made and what resources the company has used. This audit or assessment includes observations made through primary qualitative research and includes information shared by the client through meetings and interviews. This assessment delves deeply into the areas of focus related to the campaign.

Public Perception is an external analysis of the company or client that examines what the public says, thinks and feels about the company or client as a whole and related to specific topics. This type of assessment has a number of layers to it, begins with an internet search and deals with reviews of rating sites and public reviews. Examining comments on sites such as Yelp are useful at this review stage. Additionally, this is the stage when it is necessary to review media coverage, examine social media platforms for interaction and review what the feeling is that people share via word-of-mouth or on more formal channels.

External Audit or Assessment is an external review of which forces influence a company or client and can impact the focus of the campaign. These forces include but are not limited to: region and culture, weather, availability of resources, availability of supportive audiences and so on. The external audit or assessment also accounts for competitors, political client (if relevant), economic client (if relevant), persons associated with industry externally and so on. This part of the situation analysis is often difficult for people to cover comprehensively.

Within the situation analysis, there is no cross-over of content.

Example: If the focus of the campaign is children of lesser means within a community and the external audit uncovers a bias toward those children by the segment of the community that is educated, wealthy and has a surplus of means, then that description cannot be addressed in the public perception or any other sections.

SWOT ANALYSIS SECOND

Writing a Proper SWOT

To write a SWOT that easily understandable by the client, it is best to move past the block SWOT written in books to *illustrate* the connection of terms. However, a word cloud of terms does not paint an accurate picture for the client of what is the current situation (See Appendix Pages 152–153).

Carefully review each section below and the outcomes of what is needed to complete the SWOT:

Strengths are internal to the company or client and are a comprehensive view of each of the assets. The strengths can be with a particular person internal to the company or client (i.e., a strong company leader is a strength). Strengths are assets such as a new addition or innovative new lab or winning an award. Strengths can be that the company or client is recognized for having a strong corporate culture or ethical standard. You can also identify strengths that center around the history of a company such as a standard of excellence for 80 years or that it gives back to the community through partnerships or volunteer time. Strengths that are often overlooked are the support a company or client receives or the loyalty it has offered to an industry or region.

Weaknesses are internal to the company or client and are a comprehensive view of the gaps within the company. Some weaknesses often overlooked center around the people in management and leadership roles such as lack of character, ethics, or a history of poor decision making. Additional weaknesses might be a lack of growth to accommodate the need, unwillingness to progress, or be innovative in its field. Other areas of weakness are size of staffing, little or no improvements, lack of communication and other human-resource–related areas.

More weaknesses that often lead to the need for a PR campaign include inability and inefficacy of messaging, lack of understanding of the audience and improper research.

Opportunities are external to the company or client and are a comprehensive view of the prospects that lie outside the boundaries of the company or client. These opportunities are often related to many of the strengths and weaknesses, but came from external audiences. Some opportunities include a company's or client's ability to become the voice of authenticity within an industry, offer expertise, share its leadership with external resources and more. Other possible opportunities include expansion, awards, honors, partnerships and so on.

Threats are external to the company and/or clinic and are a comprehensive view of the hazards that endanger the success of the campaign and the company and/or client as a whole. Some of the threats are as simple as inclement weather, poor selection of a date or time or location, or a misfit connection to the region or audience. Some threats are more complex and center on the competition (i.e., sabotage or mudslinging), the environment (political climate or trends), or the success or failure of previous attempts. Threats can seem endless, but it's incumbent on the creators of the campaign to find threats that are relevant for the project, company, or client and help paint a picture.

Note: Unlike with the situation analysis, it is important to understand that the same focus can be addressed as both a strength and weakness and again from a different angle in the opportunities or threats.

Example: Weakness—Lack of innovation sets company in last place among competition. Threat—Company is last among competition due to lack of innovation. Opportunity—Ability to apply for innovation grant offered to companies in need of support for innovation advancement.

WORKSHEET 8A

WRITE YOUR OWN SITUATION ANALYSIS

Start with your Client Background. Just write notes of what is important to include in your written description.

_____

_____

_____

_____

_____

_____

_____

_____

_____

Next, let's write the Internal Audit/Assessment. Just write notes of what is important to include in your written description.

_____

_____

_____

_____

_____

_____

_____

_____

_____

Now let's address the Public Perception. Just write notes of what is important to include in your written description.

_____

_____

_____

_____

_____

_____

_____

_____

Next, let's write the External Audit/Assessment. Just write notes of what is important to include in your written description.

_____

_____

_____

_____

_____

_____

_____

_____

WORKSHEET 8B

SWOT ANALYSIS FOR YOUR CLIENT

Start by circling or checking some of the terms below that will help you begin writing the sections of your SWOT. After each brainstorm section, write a few bullets that you can use to begin formulating your SWOT.

STRENGTHS (Internal):

Attitude	Behavior	Creativity	Loyalty	Support	Trust
Organization	Advancement	Joy	History	Culture	
Management/ Leadership	Resources	Region	Success		

_____

_____

_____

_____

_____

_____

_____

WEAKNESS (Internal):

Attitude	Behavior	Creativity	Loyalty	Support	Trust
Organization (Within)	Advancement	History	Culture	Competition	
Management/ Leadership	Resources	Region	Expectations		

_____

_____

_____

_____

_____

_____

_____

_____

OPPORTUNITIES (External):

Industry   Competition   Climate Socio-Economics   Voices

Equity   Movements   Politics Trends   Alliances   Fun/Fear

_____

_____

_____

_____

_____

_____

_____

THREATS (External):

Industry   Competition   Climate   Socio-Economics   Voices

Equity   Movements   Politics   Trends   Alliances   Fun/Fear

_____

_____

_____

_____

_____

_____

_____

CHAPTER 9

WRITING THE PR CAMPAIGN PLAN

WRITING IS KEY

The final PR campaign is a comprehensive "document" that includes a number of individual pieces. Each of the pieces within a PR campaign is essential to making decisions, creating tactics, understanding the audiences and developing strategic evaluations and measurements. Although most PR writing is based on AP style, it is important to be flexible in your ability to write in multiple styles. The overall PR campaign plan is best if written similarly to a business plan. It is important the plan stays professional and focused on facts. This is critical in sections such as the SWOT and situation analysis. It should never seem as though the author(s) of the written campaign plan are offering analysis with any bias or negative spin, remaining neutral is best.

Persuasion is used when developing a PR campaign written plan in the sections specific to the tactics created to resolve the issue. This means that beginning with tactics and ending with recommendations, the plan can have more persuasive phrasing and word choices included to help the client choose to use the suggestions and implement the ideas.

How to Organize the Plan

Organizing the PR campaign plan should be specific to the client and the team. However, it is important to make sure the following elements are included in the final written campaign. The order for the plan must be in an order that is easy to follow and build on itself. In other words, it doesn't make logical sense to put the evaluations and measurements first when clearly that is at the end of the PR campaign.

Creating a table of contents is a way to start the organizational process. The strategy behind using the table of contents as your outline involves a risk in that anything that is not created must be removed from the table of contents before printing. This technique helps reduce another step in the overall development since creating a table of contents is almost always necessary given the comprehensive nature of the project.

A sample version of the table of contents is included in Figure 9.1, but remember each PR campaign is different and some elements may be added or removed as needed to make this individualized to the client.

Figure 9.1 Sample Table of Contents

Cover Page
Executive Summary
Table of Contents

- I. Challenge (or Problem or Opportunity)
- II. Situation Analysis
  - a. Concise picture of the client and environment
  - b. SWOT:
    - i. Strengths Weaknesses
    - ii. Opportunities Threats
- III. Target Audience
  - a. Primary and Secondary Audiences
    - iii. Demographics and Psychographics
      1. Prepackaged Audiences
      2. Opinion Leaders
  - b. Specialty Audiences
- IV. Research
  - a. Research summary
  - b. Secondary research summary
  - c. Primary research
    - i. Reference to instrument
    - ii. Methodology
    - iii. Conclusions
- V. Goal
- VI. Tactical Plan
  - a. Messages/Themes
  - b. Objectives, Strategies and Tactics
  - c. Tactical Outline (including budget)
- VII. Evaluations & Measurements
  - a. Evaluations by Objective
  - b. Measurement Scale for Client
- VIII. Recommendations (Detailed and Specific)
- IX. Appendices A-Z
  - a. Timeline
  - b. Budget
  - c. Media Plan
    - i. Media List(s)
  - d. Social Media Strategy
    - i. Platform Summary
    - ii. Platform Audit/Analysis
    - iii. Social Media Calendar
    - iv. Social Media Writing Samples
  - e. Writing Samples
    - i. Collaterals
      1. Advisory
      2. Alert
      3. Pitch
      4. Release
  - f. Design Samples
    - i. Banners/Posters
    - ii. E-vites
    - iii. Fliers
    - iv. PowerPoint
    - v. Promotional Samples
    - vi. Video Samples/Stills
  - g. Primary Research
    - i. Interview/Survey Questions
    - ii. Interview/Survey Results
    - iii. SPSS/Excel Results
    - iv. Research Correlations
  - h. Secondary Research
  - i. Reference List (A-Z, APA Format)
    - i. Original Articles
  - j. Presentation Slides

Creation of the Basics

Cover Page: The cover page should represent the design of the overall PR campaign. This can include the slogan and design elements, should include the name of the campaign itself and perhaps should include the names of the team members.

Executive Summary: The executive summary is a condensed version of the key elements of the complete PR campaign. This does not give all the tactical elements, but does explain the issue, basics of the situation analysis and SWOT, target audience analysis and research results and then gives the goal and objectives (See Appendix Page 145).

Table of Contents: Addressed previously.

Challenge: The issue statement is a one-sentence critical statement that exemplifies the root issue that the PR campaign aims to resolve. Caution to not write a statement that is negatively slanted at the organization in that it seems as though the entire organizations "fails." The statement must be clear and concise.

> *Example:* The issue of the PR campaign is the lack of public awareness and education surrounding X company's initiatives of youth education and after-school programming due to poor communication plans, disconnected social media strategies and minimal education efforts.

Situation Analysis: The situation analysis and SWOT should be written with a fact-based approach. The delivery of the SWOT, unless requested by the client, should not be delivered in a square box S, W, O, T. This technique is very challenging to read and does not allow for one of the four sections to be longer than the others. The best practice for the presentation for the SWOT is the delivery of each statement with action verbs (when possible) in bullets.

Analysis and Research

Target Audience: Writing the target audience starts with an introduction and then works through demographic descriptions with specific examples of prepackaged audiences and opinion leaders that "speak" to that specific group. This section must be written clearly to define who is the audience for the PR campaign. The target audience is best described when it paints a picture of the audience and incorporates specialty audiences and subgroups.

Research: The research section begins with an overall research introduction that includes information about the topics covered in secondary research and the methodology and results from primary research.

Secondary Research: Secondary research is sometimes referred to as a literature review. This research covers all the complimentary topics that are required to learn more about the subject matter. Secondary research should be written by weaving together supportive research materials with proper citation under subheadings of the pertinent topics. Most clients understand American Psychological Association (APA) or Modern Language Association (MLA) citation formatting for the in-text citation and reference pages.

Primary Research: The primary research section is often one of the longest sections of the written plan. The introduction explains the purpose and what type of research was utilized to attain the needed information. The sections of the research include research tool, BETA testing, methodology, results, conclusions and limitations.

Goal and Tactical Elements

Goal: The goal is usually one sentence or a few sentences that encompass the overall focus of the PR campaign. This statement stands alone and should not be combined for greater impact.

Tactical Plan: This section of the PR campaigns plan includes the explanation of the Messages and Themes. This may also be where the team chooses to include the writing and design style guides to keep everything consistent. The tactical plan also includes tactical outlines for events (which include a budget). The full tactical plan has individual sections that include each objective, with the strategies and tactics that help accomplish that goal.

Summaries and Suggestions

Evaluations and Measurements: Each of the evaluations should be connected directly to the objective that it assesses. The measurements should be created specifically to measure success or failure of that evaluation and should have a clear scale. Examples of scales are Gold, Silver and Bronze, or perhaps three emoji faces for happy, mediocre and sad. Scales can be created specifically tied to the client.

Example: An education/school project might have Red, Yellow and Green apples. A project for a show (acting, comedy, dance) might have standing ovation, applause and crickets as the scale.

Recommendations: Write the recommendations with a heavy dose of persuasion to encourage the client to continue with the PR campaign. The recommendations are also the elements that were unable to fit within the confines set by the client. These tactics are often ones that can elevate the overall PR campaign to the next level.

Appendices

When writing the appendices, remember to include the tactical elements for the client. Each appendix should be identified and labeled/divided. The contents of each section must also be labeled regarding which area is referenced or for the client's benefit. The media plan should include how to use releases, advisories and alerts properly to achieve success in the plan. The media lists should be properly labeled indicating to the client the media that are appropriate to send tactical elements to or whom to contact for specific reasons.

Each appendix might have subsections, which should also be carefully labeled and organized so as to avoid confusion for the client. Formatting is the same; therefore a client will not know the difference between two press releases unless those releases are labeled (See Appendix Pages 186–188).

WORKSHEET 9A

CREATE YOUR OWN TABLE OF CONTENTS

Number each one of the sections below to create your own table of contents draft as a starting point.

_____ Challenge

_____ Cover Page

_____ Evaluations & Measurements

_____ Executive Summary

_____ Goal

_____ Recommendations

_____ Research

_____ Situation Analysis

_____ Table of Contents

_____ Tactical Plan

_____ Target Audience

Appendices:

_____ Budget

_____ Design Samples

_____ Media List(s)

_____ Media Plan

_____ Presentation Slides

_____ Primary Research

_____ Secondary Research

_____ Social Media Strategy

_____ Tactical Outlines

_____ Timeline

_____ Writing Samples

WORKSHEET 9B

CREATE A WORKFLOW AND TIMELINE FOR WRITING THE PLAN

Although the majority of the PR campaign plans created today are worked on through the duration of an entire course or during the span of several months, the writing is often done in pieces. It is best to create a working timeline of when each person who is part of the team has their drafts and their finals completed and ready for incorporation.

It is important to make sure that the timeline for writing the plan allocates for printing or combining into one overall document for the client and allows for mistakes. The assumption should not be that everyone on the team makes each deadline and that one or more members will be late.

ITEM	DRAFT DATE	FINAL DATE	NOTE
Challenge	_____	_____	_____
Cover Page	_____	_____	_____
Evaluations & Measurements	_____	_____	_____
Executive Summary	_____	_____	_____
Goal	_____	_____	_____
Recommendations	_____	_____	_____
Research	_____	_____	_____
Situation Analysis	_____	_____	_____
Table of Contents	_____	_____	_____
Tactical Plan	_____	_____	_____
Target Audience	_____	_____	_____
Appendices			
Budget	_____	_____	_____
Design Samples	_____	_____	_____
Media List(s)	_____	_____	_____
Media Plan	_____	_____	_____
Presentation Slides	_____	_____	_____

Primary Research _____ _____ _____

Secondary Research _____ _____ _____

Social Media Strategy _____ _____ _____

Tactical Outlines _____ _____ _____

Timeline _____ _____ _____

Writing Samples _____ _____ _____

CHAPTER 10

CREATING TACTICS FROM RESEARCH AND ANALYSIS

SYNTHESIZING RESEARCH INTO A STRATEGY

Most of what has been done to this point should include the following:

- Assessing the client regarding the situation analysis, the company's strengths and weaknesses and its outward opportunities and threats

- Painting a comprehensive picture of who exactly is the primary and secondary audience for the organization that includes prepackaged audiences, opinion leaders and specialty groups

- Reviewing research already completed on related topics and extrapolating from the conclusions the information that is most valuable for this PR campaign

- Designing and executing a customized research plan to attain knowledge specific to the client and the project to guide in the deliverables and success of the overall campaign

- Creating a plan to guide the client through the phases of the campaign, how the goal is met and the expectations of each objective as it relates to elements of PR

This amount of data and information can be overwhelming. Although there is no singular way to approach sifting through this information to begin creating the PR campaign, most practitioners use the objective-based approach. This method begins by taking one objective at a time and asking the practitioner to consider which strategies might best accomplish success.

Example (Objective from Chapter 3): Increase Facebook interactivity by 20% from January 2021 to June 2021.

Using the example objective above, some possible strategies might be:

- *Create unique content with stories as the baseline.*

- *Offer exclusivity to the Facebook friends following/interacting.*

- *Collaborate with other organizations and individuals to enrich the story.*

- *Build a targeted advertising and marketing push to capitalize on the gain.*

*Note: There are more strategies; these are just a few for the sake of the example.

After all the possible strategies are listed, it is essential for the team to begin examining the information and research previously gathered for clues about what strategies might be most successful. In the target audience analysis, if it is clear that the primary audience is distrustful of advertising and marketing efforts directly from the organization, then take that into consideration. If the secondary research reveals that collaboration with influencers is highly successful on Instagram, but only moderately successful on Facebook, perhaps that is something to consider as well. If the primary research conclusions reveal that storytelling was first on their list of engagement opportunities for Facebook, then that is also something to consider.

The process is to only adopt strategies that allow for the objective to be reached within the timeframe. If the audience is not receptive or the research indicates that there has not been previous success in these areas, then it makes more logical sense to consider incorporating the strategies that the team knows will work. Each strategy has tactics that help meet the objective. Tactical elements include the written content from a social media content calendar and individual posts that reach the audience and form a connection to the audience.

Tactical Elements

Tactical elements are highly individualized to the specific client and the campaign. The challenge with creating a PR campaign, especially while in college, is fighting the urge to create the tactical pieces before the research and information gathering is complete. Many great ideas are just that, ideas with support that they will result in success. Although a PR campaign can have a few unproven elements, it is not a best practice to include too many of these elements.

It takes focus to stay on track and accomplish all the information gathering and research first, followed by strategy review and then the application and creation of tactics. Additionally, having a list of what is possible as a tactical element is helpful (See Appendix Pages 189–198).

Media Plan and Media Lists: A strategic media plan can include different pieces depending on what is best for the client. Most incorporate definitions of the pieces included as well as usage suggestions. Media plans explain the strategy for overall engagement with the press. Therefore, if the PR campaign employs an approach that is information heavy or information as needed, a simple press release and pitch to a long-term beat writer might yield the proper result. If the campaign has elements of promotion, then a more aggressive approach to garner media coverage including media engagement to create buzz may

---

Figure 10.1   Tactical Elements

Written Elements:
- Media Advisory
- Media Alert
- Media Release
- Media Pitch
- Feature Story
- Opinion Editorial

Design Elements:
- Booklet
- Brochure
- E-vite

- E-flier
- Flier
- Poster
- Presentation

Social Media Elements:
- Platform Audit
- Social Media Strategy Calendar
- Social Media Post Calendar

Event Elements:
- Tactical Outlines
- Event Plan and Budget

be necessary. Media plans also include a full calendar of deployment and media lists for local media and endemic press. These lists should include the full name and title of the press person, his/her/their email and phone number plus social media handles if possible. There are a number of services that can assist in building such lists. Cision offers a college-level service for professors and students to familiarize themselves with the products before entering the real world. Other services such as Muck Rack and Presswire also assist in building media lists and distribution as well.

Written Elements: Not every PR campaign needs several media releases, advisories and alerts. The best way to determine if a written tactical element is needed is to ask if it is newsworthy, will garner press coverage, move the narrative forward and provide needed information to the appropriate audiences. In many instances, a fewer number of well-written pieces on the suitable subject are more successful than numerous pieces sent scattershot to all media without a plan. The written elements must be tied directly to a strategy, which is tied directly to an objective. This ensures that no PR campaign will accidently have two or more releases or written pieces on the exact same subject. Written elements should all follow a standardized style guide that is created at the start of the PR campaign and approved by the client. This written style guide includes, but is not limited to, company name and usage, address, executives, slogans, jargon specific to the industry, use of AP Style and then any specific abbreviations or terms.

- Media Advisory: Often sent to a press list up to 3 months in advance or as close as 2 weeks before an event or newsworthy element. Advisories are often formatted in the Who, What, When, Where. Why and How format. I advise not using the term *How* as it is generic and often tell students that it is better to utilize specific terms like *tickets* or *attire* or *directions*. This is more specific information for the media to utilize as they disseminate information to the public.

- Media Alert: Often sent to the press within 24 hours of the newsworthy element. This is typically utilized for bigger announcements such as a road closure, cancelation of an event or even attaining a goal (i.e., reaching a sales goal or exceeding donation expectations). This often follows the same formatting as a press release.

- Press Pitch: Targeted offer for individual members of the press to garner coverage. Quality pitches are delivered via email or phone and are concise and include a strong offer and/or hook.

- Press Release: Press releases are the cornerstone of all PR campaigns as the primary method of delivering detailed information to members of the traditional press. Press releases must include the delivery of newsworthy information, a quote, a company boilerplate and contact information. Well-written press releases have a lot of information transferred to the press.

Design Elements: As with the written elements, not every PR campaign requires every form of promotional design or informational design elements. Some PR campaigns have more digital design components and others have a blend. In most PR campaigns, there are only a few pieces of design materials utilized, each with a specific purpose. The most impactful design elements are those that mix together function and design. It is important when creating any design pieces to take the time to create a style guide. The design style guide includes, but is not limited to, logo slick, color palette, vector graphics, image bank, font options and more.

- Brochure: These are hand-held design pieces that must have a fold to be considered a brochure. With older audiences, brochures are very effective and if designed properly are very desirable in delivering messaging.

- Fliers: Most often, fliers are 8.5"x11" or smaller in size and are often handed out, included in mailers or disseminated in person. Fliers are either one color or full color depending on the budget and are often the most cost-effective design option as it can be created at a copy company.

- Posters: The smallest poster size is usually 11"x17" and the most common size is 24"x36". Posters are almost always full color and a more long-term and expensive option.

- Table Cards or Tents: With promotions, promotional pieces that are set up on tables are easy ways to deliver information and messaging and can be interactive.

Social Media Elements: Social media is essential in any modern PR campaign. The tactical elements in a social media strategy start with auditing the platforms the company currently has live. The second part of the strategy is to create a strategic calendar that includes elements such as birthdays, holidays, industry days and connections to days such as #MotivationalMondays, #ThrowbackThursdays, #FunFactFridays and so on. As with the written elements and the design elements, it is best practices to create a social media style guide. This style guide includes, but is not limited to handles for each social media platform, a hashtag bank, image cropping suggestions and more.

- Part I: Social media audit is an in-depth examination of each platform that the organization currently utilizes. Within the review, I suggest that students review at least 3 months' worth of content and from this examination, students should be able to determine the tone of the communication, the audience and the breakdown of how much content is educational, entertaining, informational or promotional. This audit must be detailed and include a breakdown of the audience for each platform, review of the current content and should not include any suggestions or ideas.

- Part II: Social media strategic calendar is a set of ideas based on what the organization SHOULD be doing to reach the set objectives. This means that garnering more followers is a differing approach than advancing interactivity. The strategic calendar must consider including the following:

  1. Anniversaries (for the organization or industry)

  2. Birthdays (of related people, e.g., Edward Bernays)

  3. Holidays (national, international etc.)

  4. Industry Days (National Dance Day, Adopt-a-Pet Day or Hug your dog Day etc.)

  5. Trending Days (Motivational Mondays, Fun Fact Friday, TBT etc.)

This section also provides direction on how to utilize each social media platform such as how often to post, when to post something that is evergreen versus part of the schedule and so forth.

- Part III: Social media sample posts are done for each day of a calendar year and across all platforms. It is BEST practices to not post the same content on multiple platforms for the same day unless it is day specific, such as a holiday or birthday. The expectation here is providing as much detail and sampling as possible for the client. No content should ever be provided to the client that they cannot post, which includes imagery. If there is not a viable image to use that is appropriate for the client and free to use, then writing the word SAMPLE across the image in white text with a slightly lower opacity is the best option.

Note: Social media content is more challenging to master than people realize for an organization. The key to creating quality content is to examine what type of engagement the audience responds to. This process often takes months and is a process. Imagery is always key as pictures are easy for people to react to in a positive way and interact with.

Keys for success include:

- Facebook: Tagging companies and individuals to grow your audience. Creating content that allows for engagement at a grassroots level that creates a genuine community of people.

- Instagram: Imagery is so important as that is why people are on Instagram. Tagging and using # within the content so that your work can be searched help grow the audience.

- Pinterest: Imagery and information is key because Pinners are loyal to sources of information.

- Snapchat: Content for a company must be developed with a strategic plan and messaging to include key words.

- Twitter: Great tweets have a strong message with at least two # embedded in the content that are searchable. Twitters need to engage with the audience and start a conversation.

Event Elements: Not all PR campaigns require the creation and execution of special events. The implementation of an event means that the client has something specifically designed and deployed just for the purpose of meeting the needs of the objectives. When creating an event plan, there many considerations including budget, timeline, event description, audience, takeaways and more. It is important for events to serve the purpose of accomplishing several positive strides while possibly attached to more than one objective. Often events are time consuming and expensive; therefore, it makes sense that each event connects to a few objectives.

Checking Your Strategies and Tactics

Although there is no magic number of tactical elements that each strategy must have to achieve success and no specific number of strategies an objective must have, it should be comprehensive without being redundant. The best PR campaigns are innovative, thorough and directed and/or focused. It is important for the PR campaign to have a mix of several different types of tactical elements. The diversity of elements ensures that there is something for everyone and the messaging will reach every person in the Target Audience. Limiting the tactical pieces might have consequences that impact other parts of the PR campaign that needed audience saturation and message repetition as a way for the message to be absorbed. Tactical elements can be used for multiple strategies and to achieve multiple objectives.

Example: A feature story for the website could be used for a digital storytelling strategy and for an informational strategy to the public.

A spectacular idea might only fit with one strategy, but might move that strategy drastically forward, thus making it a viable tactic. After each tactical element is considered, a final list of the tactics and strategies is created for each objective. Be careful that each multiuse tactic is written identically no matter where in the PR campaign it is used to avoid confusion on there being two similar tactical pieces as opposed to the same piece used for multiple purposes. Clarity is key when outlining the overall PR campaign.

WORKSHEET 10A

CREATING STRATEGIES FOR YOUR OBJECTIVES

Objective 1: _____

_____

_____

Possible Strategies:

- _____
- _____
- _____
- _____
- _____
- _____

Objective 2: _____

_____

_____

Possible Strategies:

- _____
- _____
- _____
- _____
- _____
- _____

Objective 3: _____

_____

_____

Possible Strategies:

- _____
- _____
- _____
- _____
- _____
- _____

Objective 4: _____

_____

_____

Possible Strategies:

- _____
- _____
- _____
- _____
- _____
- _____

Objective 5: _____

_____

_____

Possible Strategies:

- _____
- _____
- _____

- _____
- _____
- _____

Objective 6: _____

_____

_____

Possible Strategies:

- _____
- _____
- _____
- _____
- _____
- _____

Objective 7: _____

_____

_____

Possible Strategies:

- _____
- _____
- _____
- _____
- _____
- _____

WORKSHEET 10B

OBJECTIVES, STRATEGIES, AND TACTICS

Use the following to envision what tactics support the strategies that align with achieving success for each objective. Repeat this technique as a way to start the brainstorming process.

Objective 1: _____

_____

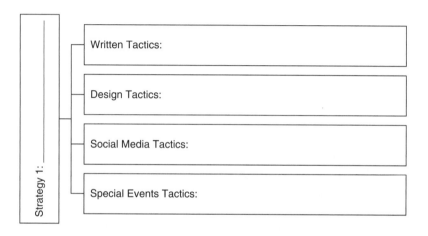

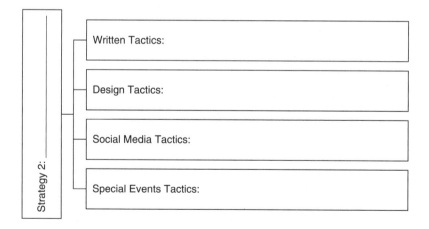

Objective 2: _____

_____

Strategy 1: _____

Written Tactics:

Design Tactics:

Social Media Tactics:

Special Events Tactics:

Strategy 2: _____

Written Tactics:

Design Tactics:

Social Media Tactics:

Special Events Tactics:

WORKSHEET 10C

BRAINSTORM OF SOCIAL MEDIA CONTENT

Key words used on Facebook:

_____

_____

_____

_____

_____

Key people and organizations to tag on Facebook:

_____

_____

_____

_____

_____

Key words used on Instagram:

_____

_____

_____

_____

_____

Key # used on Instagram:

_____

_____

_____

_____

_____

Key words used on Twitter:

_____

_____

_____

_____

Key # used on Twitter:

_____

_____

_____

_____

Pin ideas for Pinterest:

_____

_____

_____

_____

Snap ideas for Snapchat:

_____

_____

_____

_____

AUDIT NOTES

Only answer the following for the platforms that your client has:

- Who is the target audience for Facebook?

  _____

  _____

- Who is the target audience for Instagram?

  _____

  _____

- Who is the target audience for Pinterest?

  _____

  _____

- Who is the target audience for Snapchat?

  _____

  _____

- Who is the target audience for Twitter?

  _____

  _____

What do you see as trends for:

- Facebook

  _____

  _____

- Instagram

  _____

  _____

- Pinterest

  _____

  _____

- Snapchat

  _____

  _____

- Twitter

  _____

  _____

What are the successes the organization has on:

- Facebook

  _____

  _____

- Instagram

  _____

  _____

- Pinterest

  _____

  _____

- Snapchat

  _____

  _____

- Twitter

  _____

  _____

What are the failures the organization has on:

- Facebook

  _____

  _____

- Instagram

  _____

  _____

- Pinterest

  _____

  _____

- Snapchat

  _____

  _____

- Twitter

  _____

  _____

CALENDAR NOTES

Only write notes for your client:
Anniversaries (for the organization or industry)

- Facebook

  _____

  _____

- Instagram

  _____

  _____

- Pinterest

  _____

  _____

- Snapchat

  _____

  _____

- Twitter

  _____

  _____

Birthdays (of related people, e.g., Edward Bernays)

- Facebook

  _____

  _____

- Instagram

  _____

  _____

- Pinterest

  _____

  _____

- Snapchat

  _____

  _____

- Twitter

  _____

  _____

Holidays (national, international, etc.)

- Facebook

  _____

  _____

- Instagram

  _____

  _____

- Pinterest

  _____

  _____

- Snapchat

  _____

  _____

- Twitter

  _____

  _____

Industry Days (National Dance Day, Adopt-a-Pet Day or Hug your dog Day, etc.)

- Facebook

  _____

  _____

- Instagram

  _____

  _____

- Pinterest

  _____

  _____

- Snapchat

  _____

  _____

- Twitter

  _____

  _____

Trending Days (Motivational Mondays, Fun Fact Friday, TBT, etc.)

- Facebook

  _____

  _____

- Instagram

  _____

  _____

- Pinterest

  _____

  _____

- Snapchat

  _____

  _____

- Twitter

  _____

  _____

CHAPTER 11

EVALUATION AND MEASUREMENTS

WHY EVALUATE? WHEN, HOW, AND WITH WHAT MEASUREMENTS?

Evaluation

Evaluation: Originally proposed as part of the Public Relations plan created by the *founders* of modern PR such as Edward Bernays, Ivy Lee and more in the early 1900s, evaluation is more than reviewing the success or failure of an overall campaign. The RACE (Research, Action, Communication and Evaluation) framework model places great importance on both research and evaluation; as does the ROSIE model, which stands for Research, Objectives, Strategies and planning, Implementation and Evaluation. Evaluation is at the core of all PR campaigns as it allows for the practitioner to monitor the success or failure of the tactical elements as they are deployed and utilized by the audience.

Edward Bernays is known for some of the original landmark campaigns, such as the "Torches of Freedom" campaign with Lucky Strike and the Ivory Soap sculpting campaign. During both campaigns, Bernays was able to evaluate the success of the campaigns through less formal measurements, but they still were invaluable in proving the direction and success of each campaign. Throughout the 1900s, as campaigns for products, services, people, places, movements and ideas were deployed, evaluation was a key factor to keeping the campaign on track and achieving success.

The Importance of Evaluation

Communications can be tied to the bottom line. When significant financial investments are made to support a campaign, it is essential to determine in real time if each objective is met as it is deployed. It is unreasonable to think that spending $10,000 in creative, plus advertising and hosting a mini-event would automatically garner the results the client desires. You have to create specific evaluation methods and determine the measurement tools used as a scale to determine success or failure.

A reason organizations place such little emphasis on the evaluation is that it is often difficult to determine the economic benefit of the PR function. This is a falsity in that PR campaigns efforts are easily connected to the bottom line if the person creating the evaluation can convert the impressions and engagement on social media or real-life interactions and experiences with a dollar amount.

It is crucial for communication and PR departments to show results to keep their allocation of money and staff. Additionally, most agencies must demonstrate success to keep clients, earn new business and demonstrate both proactivity and attention to detail.

The Difficulty of Evaluation

Public Relations campaigns produce *soft* benefits that are intangible and difficult to measure in some cases. A campaign with an objective to alter a person's perception of something may take three phases to show accomplishment and it might be a challenge to document immediate results. What is easier to evaluate is a reduction in consumption within a given space.

Two types of *evidence* are often used, anecdotal and empirical. Both have flaws and benefits.

- Anecdotal Evidence: A form of criteria that can be used to measure the results of a public relations campaign. An example would be to include an informal discussion with a journalist who is in a position to evaluate the organization's performance.

- Empirical Evidence: The effectiveness of PR campaigns is difficult to evaluate empirically. Persuasion is usually a subtle process and people rarely remember how they receive the information on which they base their decisions.

The Evaluation Process

There is no one simple, all-encompassing method by which PR programs can be evaluated. The most effective approach is to combine a number of different methods. The best *plan* is to create a timeline within each objective and set up regularly spaced increments during which the company will go through the evaluation process using preset measurements that are too specific to the objective.

Preliminary proposal stage:

- Ongoing Evaluation: Describes the methods that are used to adjust or fine-tune the program while it is in progress.
  Not possible in all cases.

- Summative Evaluation: Describes how the program will be evaluated after its completion.
  Listing of the methods by which one plans to measure the results.
  Written in future tense.

- Formative Evaluation: Describes what is learned from the program, especially during the summative evaluation and serves as the starting point for future programs.
  Only found in the final version of the program book.

Evaluation Equals Success or Failure

Most people believe that performing an evaluation is the exact moment when the creator finds out if the campaign is successfully achieving what the creators hoped or if the group just spent time and money on a dead project. That is a fallacy. Evaluation just helps the creators check to see if indeed the campaign is on the correct path. If and only if success is easily trackable, then the creators can look toward the future. If the creators find that some elements are still unable to achieve a level of success, an ongoing evaluation allows for creators to adjust the campaign to hopefully offer a more successful path (See Appendix 183–185).

The Importance of Measurements

Measurements are the *scale* by which a tactical element or elements within a campaign are graded to determine success, mediocrity or failure. These are the same measurements used for a tactic regardless of *when* in the campaign timeline the measurement is deployed.

Example: In the campaign, it is determined that the team must launch a Twitter account because the client only has Facebook and is not great at taking pictures. The objective this tactic supports is to grow a larger audience and engage with the audience.

Measurements are developed in conjunction with the client and the creators of the campaign. The measurements need to be realistic, attainable and logical. Launching a Twitter account with zero followers and hoping for that account to hit 10,000 followers in 3 months is unlikely. It's important when setting measurements to understand the client, the market and the industry. These three pieces of knowledge allow the creators to outline a reasonable set of measurements.

Measurements are best when made for specific objectives. See Figure 11.1, used as a measurement for launching a new social media platform for a local Special Olympics chapter. The colors are chosen to represent the medals given to their athletes at the completion of their *games* in each division. This measurement was used six times within one calendar year. The measurement tool was not changed; it was set to reach the end objective of 7,500 followers within 1 year through grassroots engagement tactics and solid content (See Appendix 183–185).

Some other forms of evaluations and measurements are also included in the following section.

A Figure or Infographic Is the Best Way to Depict Information for Measurements. You Create a Scale (Bronze, Silver, Gold) and the Measurements of Success or Failure and the Timeline. The Most Creative Way to Provide This Information Is by Using Imagery.

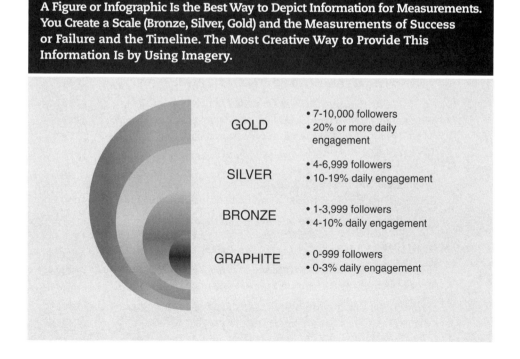

GOLD
- 7-10,000 followers
- 20% or more daily engagement

SILVER
- 4-6,999 followers
- 10-19% daily engagement

BRONZE
- 1-3,999 followers
- 4-10% daily engagement

GRAPHITE
- 0-999 followers
- 0-3% daily engagement

Evaluation Criteria and Research Methods

- Analysis of Media Coverage
  - Oldest, most traditional method by which results can be measured (i.e., counting clips)
  - Least meaningful
    - Shows media activity, but not progress toward the goal
    - Considered superficial and misleading
    - Not all recipients of the publication in which the clip was found read the articles in question
    - Reflects mainly short-term results
  - Some companies use media monitoring services
    - Search for either verbatim mentions or key words and phrases
    - Deliver monthly packets of clips
      - Distributed internally to keep key departments informed
  - Factors to consider when analyzing media clips:
    - Location
    - Tone
    - Potential Audience
    - Length
    - Context
    - Content
  - More meaningful method is to look for key messages mentioned in mass media

- Advertising Equivalency
  - A form of measurement that is popular but controversial
  - If a positive story appears in the newspaper, a value is measured by determining how much it would cost to purchase a display ad of that same size
  - Similar technique for TV news (time rather than size)
  - Shortcomings to this technique:
    - Inability to quantify negative media
    - Inability to determine the value of a front-page news article
    - Unable to account mentions on editorial pages

- Audience Feedback
  - Includes an analysis of the sales leads and feedback gathered from customers and event participants through comments cards, toll-free numbers and so on.
  - Not all organizations have sales leads, but they can keep up with responses.

- Message Recall
  - Viewers of a TV program are asked to describe which commercial messages they remember after the program has concluded.
  - Drawback is that it is often applied in the private settings (i.e., focus groups), where attention is already higher than normal.

- Financial Indicators
  - Why are consumers buying or not buying?
  - Why are donors increasing or decreasing the levels of their gifts?
- Customer Response Data
  - The responses used for evaluations individuals provide through comment cards or online questionnaires.
- Clues in Cyberspace
  - Organizations can learn what customers are saying about a company's products, services, ads and so on. by accessing a variety of other sites
    - For example, Yahoo.com links more than 140 consumer comment sites
  - Sites vary greatly in credibility
  - Opinions are subject to hype, exaggeration and falsity
- Before-and-After Comparison
  - Involves measuring change in:
    - Attitudes and Behaviors
    - Observable Behaviors

Tracking the Case

- Ongoing Evaluation:
  - The teams meet every two weeks during the implementation phase.
  - Decide on any minor adjustments that need to be made and act accordingly.
- Summative Evaluation:
  - Measure the level of achievement for the process objectives, informational objectives and outcome objectives.

WORKSHEET 11A

DEVELOPING PROPER EVALUATIONS FOR A CAMPAIGN

Write objective below (from Chapter 3):

_____

_____

_____

_____

_____

_____

_____

_____

What are the best *times* to evaluate this objective? Come up with at least two to four specific dates during actual timeline of the execution of the campaign.

1. _____

2. _____

3. _____

4. _____

5. _____

What specifically should you be evaluating within the objective? Example: In PR tactics (sending out a PR advisory, release and pitch combination), what is the best evaluation to consider?

_____

_____

_____

_____

_____

_____

_____

_____

Example of an evaluation for a PR campaign regarding tactical elements:
Evaluation of PR tactical materials to garner press coverage for ____ organization on ____ (date) of ____ (month) of ____ (year).

Now you write one evaluation for the PR campaign you are creating. Make sure you write it specific to the objective and specific to a *plot* on the overall timeline. Be careful that this corresponds with something big the campaign has planned or something significant.

_____

_____

_____

_____

_____

_____

_____

_____

WORKSHEET 11B

CREATING SCALES THAT ARE ADJUSTABLE BUT FAIR

To begin, start with what within the campaign is being measured:

_____

_____

_____

_____

_____

_____

_____

Now, determine what makes three to four levels ranging from the highest level of success to the lowest level of failure. If you make four levels, make three even levels and one that is smaller. It's best if you make the smallest level the *extreme failure* as no one wants to be in that category, but if a tactic ends up in the *super failure* zone, then both the creator and client know it genuinely did not work.

Let's create some levels:

HIGHEST	MIDDLE	LOW	LOWEST
_____	_____	_____	_____
_____	_____	_____	_____
_____	_____	_____	_____
_____	_____	_____	_____

For each level, you need to create sets of scales 10–8, 7–5, 4–2, 1–0 or whatever is appropriate for what is being measured.

Examples: In PR, you can measure clips of articles, mentions and so on. In social media you can measure followers, likes, comments and other meaningful engagement.

Many times, it is fun to use key phrases or something that is meaningful to the client to help with the scales. It makes measuring and evaluating less *scary* and also helps them remember what the terms mean, without using words like success and failure.

Examples: In a PR campaign created for the DJ Irie Foundation, the students in a PR Campaigns class created measurements: Standing Ovation (Highest), Applause (Middle), Snaps (Low) and Crickets (Lowest). In another class the students created a PR campaign for a celebrity food and wine festival centered around grilling and the measurements were: Well Done (Highest), Medium Well (Middle), Medium (Low) and Rare (Lowest).

Now you create some samples of creative phrases you can use for your client.

HIGHEST	MIDDLE	LOW	LOWEST
_____	_____	_____	_____
_____	_____	_____	_____
_____	_____	_____	_____
_____	_____	_____	_____

CHAPTER 12

WHAT DOES THAT MEAN?

Recommendations: It is possible that many people believe that the tactical elements created in Chapters 9 and 10 are all recommendations to the client of what a company should do. For the purposes of a complete campaign, that is not the definition used of recommendations. The definition for recommendations is anything that can benefit a campaign that is unable to be included because of reasons beyond the scope of the project.

Reasoning for Recommendations?

Recommendations are often developed when creating the tactical elements or strategic plan. During the brainstorming process, some ideas are developed that do not end up fitting the criteria for the campaign. This means the idea may cost too much and not fit with the constraints of the budget, it might not fit the primary target audience or it might not work toward one of the objectives. These are all reasons a team may choose not to use an idea and therefore, the idea is "tabled" for later consideration.

Ideas that are not an obvious fit should go through a second review for consideration before they are eliminated. The first review should be to consider if the idea can be shifted to fit into the budget, touch on the target audience or attack one of the objectives. If with a slight adjustment, the idea/tactic is viable, then this is moved into the category of a workable idea/tactic.

If the first review is still not viable, then the idea/tactic should be considered for a recommendation. If the idea is thought to be of significant value to the future success of the campaign, then it is worthwhile to spend a little time developing the idea/tactic. This evolution from idea to future option is a necessary step to provide to a client.

Campaigns do not end when the calendar date ends on the last tactical piece, if done well. Most campaigns can live on for months and years after its initially intended calendar run. If the campaign's success continues to grow, thus prompting a reason to keep the campaign running, then recommendations become an important future tool. These ideas are often adopted and executed with an extended budget, timeline, audience or additional objectives to accommodate for growth and success.

Organizing and Writing Recommendations

Many *lists* of ideas for recommendations are easily grouped by topic, audience or plot on the timeline. It is important for a client that recommendations are just as clear and demonstrable as the tactics outline in the plan. Most client feedback reveals that they are most *confused* by when and how to use recommendations.

When writing the final recommendations for clients, it's best to organize them for the client with a schedule and connected to objectives. Putting the recommendations first that have the most timely additions to the campaign is always best.

When writing the recommendations, there are a number of methods. Some opt for the simple method of just including the idea, but this does not provide enough detail for the client to activate the recommendation when the time comes. Some opt to create full tactical outlines, which seems excessively detailed given that the client may not deploy the recommendation. This is one of those moments in which the best course is usually somewhere in the *middle*, which means to create a recommendation with enough detail to explain what to do, but not so much that it is excessive (See Appendix Page 169).

Below is an outline of the formatting that seems the most generic and universal for all clients:

RECOMMENDATION TITLE IN BOLD ALL CAPS

Objective: Connection to which objective

Timeline: Dates to start, hit specific milestones and complete the tactic

Description: Details here on what to do to complete this tactical piece, which includes resources and cost when possible

Example:

CREATE VOICE-ENABLED SKILL WITH GENERAL COMPANY INFORMATION

Objective: Develop three new methods to reach target audience through digital and new media platforms to educate public within 6 months.

Timeline: After 6 months of the objective, this recommendation begins after the first three platforms are deployed and the content is fine-tuned through user feedback. Create at 5 months, launch at 6 months.

Description: Create a script for Google and Amazon voice-enabled devices to communicate with customers about general information about the company, services and new offerings. Depending on the depth and scope of what this *skill* includes, the cost is $5,500 to $7,500 using a local tech company that has the resources to help create voice-enabled content.

Restraint Required

The number of recommendations is entirely dependent on how many tactics a team has that are listed during the brainstorming phase and are not used in the execution of the campaign. It is conceivable that the list of recommendations could have as many tactical elements as the campaign itself; however, this is not advisable. Many PR professionals believe that offering too many recommendations simply gives the client a list of options after the prescribed length of the campaign simply negates any reason for the client to renew a contract or ask for additional support. Another school of thought is that providing a solid array of recommendations gives the client some ideas of what other services they might need to add on and therefore actually builds the idea of more work, a contract extension or revision of the timeline.

As with all things, restraint and moderation are likely the best course of action. Once the brainstorming list has been completed and the tactics for the full campaign are selected and tactical outlines created, then the remaining items should be reviewed. Those items that aid to progress the objectives and help meet the overall goal should be carefully considered. If the tactical idea is something that could benefit the long-term outcomes of the campaign, then it should be developed into a recommendation.

There is no magic number that any client is expected (unless otherwise denoted in the contract), rather it is just that all ideas not included in the confines of the campaign are carefully considered. Restraint in providing the client with every single idea and every single possibility is key. This is where having a few level-headed team members is crucial to the success of the overall campaign. These individuals are expected to always refocus the conversation on what the idea contributes to the overall goal and how the idea furthers to meet objectives.

It is natural, almost innate, for everyone on the team to want to give the client a *rainbow* of every other idea, but again, restraint is key. Careful curation of the ideas, without ego attached, is necessary to deliver the best overall project. This means omitting ideas that clearly have no ability to ever come to fruition, ideas that are perhaps too costly or could have too high of a risk factor.

The worksheet should help work through ideas. If each person in the team creates his/her/their own list and then that is cross-referenced to determine which ideas were most valuable, this should help create the final list of recommendations.

WORKSHEET 12A

DEVELOPING A LIST OF RECOMMENDATIONS

Part I:
Transfer the ideas from the worksheets in Chapters 9 and 10 that are NOT utilized in the PR campaign to meet one of the objectives. (Use additional pages as needed.)

_____	_____	_____
_____	_____	_____
_____	_____	_____
_____	_____	_____
_____	_____	_____
_____	_____	_____
_____	_____	_____
_____	_____	_____
_____	_____	_____
_____	_____	_____
_____	_____	_____
_____	_____	_____

Part II:
Divide up the ideas above into categories for consideration as viable recommendations:

*FITS WITH OBJECTIVES:

_____	_____	_____
_____	_____	_____
_____	_____	_____
_____	_____	_____

*MEETS GOAL:

_____	_____	_____
_____	_____	_____
_____	_____	_____

*FITS WITHIN BUDGET:

_____	_____	_____
_____	_____	_____
_____	_____	_____

*PROVIDES ADDED VALUE:

_____ _____ _____
_____ _____ _____
_____ _____ _____

IDEAS THAT ARE TOO COSTLY TO TIME CONSUMING:

_____ _____ _____
_____ _____ _____
_____ _____ _____

ARE TOO COMPLEX OR DIFFICULT TO EVER BE COMPLETED:

_____ _____ _____
_____ _____ _____

ARE TOO SIMILAR TO TACTICS ALREADY EXECUTED IN THE CAMPAIGN:

_____ _____ _____
_____ _____ _____

Part III:
Write the ideas that made it to the first four categories with the * in the title here.

_____ _____ _____
_____ _____ _____
_____ _____ _____
_____ _____ _____
_____ _____ _____

This is your FINAL list of recommendations for consideration. You and your team should cross-reference Part III of each of your work sheets.

Write the list of FINAL ideas that you and your teammates agree should be written up as recommendations for the client. Try to create some group names for these. Some examples of group names include

- Social Media Recommendations
- Digital/Social Recommendations
- Storytelling Recommendations
- Video Recommendations
- Live-Event Recommendations

Group Name _____:

_____   _____   _____

_____   _____   _____

Group Name _____:

_____   _____   _____

_____   _____   _____

Group Name _____:

_____   _____   _____

_____   _____   _____

CHAPTER 13

PRESENTING TO THE CLIENT

FINAL CLIENT PRESENTATIONS

After months and months of working on a PR campaign, it all comes down to creating the perfect client presentation. Most people prefer just to have their work speak for itself, but the reality is that most executives want to have a culminating presentation. This presentation is the ONE opportunity for the team to present what they have developed to resolve the issue creatively using analysis and research to design tactical pieces applicable for the audience to meet the goal.

Basic Rules for Creating a Presentation

There is a lot of discussion about what is the best way to give a presentation. After reviewing a number of possibilities, the following suggestions are a compilation of the best practices:

- **SPEAKERS:** It is best to have between two and five speakers who each write and memorize their own scripts. Ideally, each person covers a full section of the presentation. This eliminates the possibility of repetition or crossover.

- **PRESENTATION:** Slides or visuals of some sort are always preferred as opposed to just straight speaking. The use of PowerPoint, Prezi, Keynote and Google Slides are all options to create dynamic presentations. Ideally the presentation has enough information to get the point across, but not too much information that every word is on the visuals.

- **TIMING:** As always, timing really is everything. Most people agree that 20 minutes is the perfect amount of time for an in-depth presentation. This is supported by the fact that competitions in which presentations are the final determination only allocate for a maximum of 20 minutes with additional time for questions and answers.

- **SUPPLEMENTS:** The presentation is only as good as what *else* the client has to preview. It is important to offer some additional display items. This includes, but it not limited to, posters, press materials, promotional materials, videos, displays and so on.

Frame Working the Presentation

A final client presentation has several different components that all have to come together. It is important for everyone to feel as though he/she/they have a role in making this presentation a success. The chart below is broken into two areas, both of which are essential to achieve a succinct and balanced presentation where everyone has a part.

It is best to make sure that each person involved in the class and/or project gets to play to his/her/their strengths. If a person is forced into a role, it is likely that that the entire project will suffer because one person is not giving his/her/their best. Be sure that each person has a defined role and specific responsibilities on which he/she/they are evaluated (in a class this might be tied to a grade, but in a real campaign project, this might be tied to a promotion, raise or bonus).

Speakers and Professionalism

The role of a speaker is more than just a matter of if he/she/they can memorize a few words and say them on cue. The questions to ask are:

- Are they believable?

- Do they instill confidence in what they are saying?

- Are they charming and engaging to the client and audience?

- Will they act professionally?

The reality is that people who simply memorize lines are often not felt to be invested and therefore are not *believable* as speakers. This is why in PR it's a best practice to have a spokesperson who actually uses the products or services—the same concept applies. The speakers who are selected have to be invested in a positive outcome, which translates as coming across as genuine.

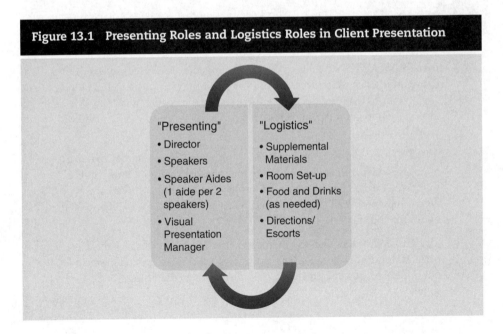

Figure 13.1 Presenting Roles and Logistics Roles in Client Presentation

"Presenting"
- Director
- Speakers
- Speaker Aides (1 aide per 2 speakers)
- Visual Presentation Manager

"Logistics"
- Supplemental Materials
- Room Set-up
- Food and Drinks (as needed)
- Directions/ Escorts

As mentioned previously in the section, all speakers should write their own scripts and therefore should be experts on the material. When a speaker puts his/her/their own words in the script, the content is more authentic and less robotic, it is also much easier for the speaker to memorize the content and deliver it with feeling.

Professionalism goes beyond just the delivery of the words, it also comes across in the physical appearance of those presenting, eye contact, facial expressions and movement when speaking. Best practices suggest that presentations of three or more should coordinate their attire to *match* so that one person's attire doesn't draw attention. This means that perhaps everyone agrees to wear all black or that everyone agrees to wear black and white in simple patterns (meaning no animal prints or geometric designs). This is easy for college students and is gender neutral.

Rehearsals are also a best practices suggestion. Collectively, it seems that at least three or four rehearsals are best, but the more the better as it only fine-tunes the delivery. During the rehearsal times, each student should be present and working on his/her/their contributions to the final presentation to the client. Other members of the class present during rehearsals who are in supportive roles can also serve as the *client* and audience while taking breaks. This provides a makeshift audience and gives feedback during the rehearsal process.

> *Example:* Someone who is a *Speaker Aide* should be at the rehearsal to take notes on the first few days of rehearsals for the speakers. If that speaker needs to have more emphasis in parts or is forgetting words in areas or is too fast or two slow, the Speaker Aides assist the speaker in working through his/her/their individual problems and polishing the performance.

Creating the Atmosphere and Presentation

Setting the stage for a professional presentation is key. If everyone feels this is *only for a grade* then neither the students, nor the professor or the client have enough invested into the outcomes. However, if everyone agrees that this is a professional project and that the intention is to utilize and implement this work, the stakes are higher and everyone has the same focus.

Ambiance and Atmosphere

Selecting the appropriate presentation space is also very important. No one wants to work on the PR campaign for months, just to walk into the final client presentation and have it be such that no one can hear him/her/them or be so distracted by outside influences that he/she/they only retain 30% of what is said. When selecting the best location, consider the following factors:

- Is the location quiet with an obvious central area of focus?

- Is the location easy to access (considering security, directions, signage etc.)?

- Does the space have the appropriate technology to support the presentation?

- Does the location allow for supportive materials to be added to customize the presentation?

Many times, applying simple hospitality techniques make all the difference. Offering attendees, a light snack, something to drink or even better, something relevant to the project is always best practices. If say the project is for a nonprofit focused on after-school programming for youth in areas where food is an issue for young people, then making sure that is used in the theme for the food service.

Example: With the above client, the snacks might be *brown bag* mini-lunches similar to what is offered to students in the program.

Many of the issues that can turn a great presentation into a bad presentation have nothing to do with content. Think about the following issues:

- Access/Security
- Acoustics
- Deliverables
- Food service/setup
- Lighting
- Noise
- Seating
- Time of day/night
- Traffic and transportation
- Widows (views of streets/people)

Presentation

The presentation outline must be customized for the client. The slides should be designed to match the PR campaign regarding color palette and design elements. Slides should be custom rather than templates provided by PowerPoint, Prezi, Keynote and so on. The best presentations are ones in which it looks like every single detail is customized. This demonstrates to the client that all work is original to this presentation.

The outline for the presentation should follow the flow of information. Each presentation team must decide which flow is best. The below example is a good start to begin the discussion and editing process:

Introduction	1 min.
Issue Statement	1 min.
SWOT and Situation Analysis, Target Audience	2.5 min.
Research	4 min.
Goal	1 min.
Objectives	2 min.
Public Relations Tactics	*5 min. (max)
Social Media Tactics	*4 min. (max)
Special Events Tactics (if applicable)	*3 min. (max)
Evaluations & Measurements	2 min.
Recommendations	2.5 min.
Questions (Not added to 25-minute total)	

*Total time for all three tactical sections is 9 minutes.

In the design of the slides, students can use transition slides to break up the content and move from topic to topic. It is also possible to use dynamic slides with movement. Be critical of the team during this phase to ensure that all the most important content is shared.

Determine which slides include imagery, infographics and videos. It is important to denote that it is fine to have slides that only have samples of the tactical work or links to created work, but be sure to account for this in the timing of the project.

Example, if the project calls for a redesign or the creation of a website, then a link to the new website is a wonderful example of a completed tactical element. However, a tour if the entire website might not fit within the time constraints.

WORKSHEET 13A

CREATING A BASIC OUTLINE FOR YOUR PRESENTATION

PRESENTATION ROLES:

Possible presentation directors

_____   _____   _____

Final presentation director _____

Possible speakers

_____   _____   _____

_____   _____   _____

_____   _____   _____

_____   _____   _____

Final speakers

_____   _____   _____

_____   _____   _____

Possible speaker aides

_____   _____   _____

_____   _____   _____

Final speaker aides

_____   _____   _____

_____   _____   _____

Possible visual presentation manager

_____   _____   _____

Final presentation visual presentation manager _____

The following are responsible for supplemental materials

_____   _____   _____

_____   _____   _____

The following are responsible for room setup

_____   _____   _____

The following are responsible for food and drinks

_____   _____   _____

The following are responsible for escorting/directing guests

_____   _____   _____

Slide Templates (Design):

Using the empty slide templates below, draw some designs that incorporate where to use the logo, design elements and colors that the teams have included in the style guide for the campaign.

Slide Templates (Content):

Using the empty slide templates below, write on the slides your content outline (from the outline above). Number the slides and if there should be more than one slide with continuous content on it, number those as such.

Example: Objectives (7–8).

PUBLIC RELATIONS
CAMPAIGN

TABLE OF CONTENTS

Irie Foundation Special Events: Executive Summary

The students of Dr. Maria Scott's Public Relations Campaigns course created a comprehensive public relations campaign for Irie Music Groups, specifically Irie Foundation and Irie Weekend. Learning objectives for this course included the creation of a professional written plan, as well as an oral and visual presentation to formally propose the campaign to the client. These learning objectives were achieved by conducting thorough primary and secondary research, developing a coherent brand design, outlining strategic tactics and organizing an oral and visual presentation. Creating this campaign provided students the opportunity to work in a team-based environment and learn to value each other's contributions by providing honest and reflective feedback. Students learned how to effectively brainstorm and collaborate, maximizing individual strengths and weaknesses while working together to achieve one end goal.

The team conducted a research plan composed of both primary and secondary research. News and scholarly articles were compiled and analyzed to aid in the future success of programming for Irie Foundation. The team researched successful nonprofit programming, factors that promote effective learning in students, nonprofit marketing strategies and Irie Foundation competitors.

After conducting secondary research, our team conducted primary research in the form of interviews to help get an idea of our target audience's knowledge of the Foundation, opinion toward its mission, volunteering habits and programming preferences for their children. These interviews, including questions about the respondents' demographics, were administered in person and the data was compiled and analyzed to determine the results and steer the direction of our objectives for the campaign.

The team then used its findings to begin crafting specific objectives to increase engagement for Irie Foundation and Irie Rhythms Academy among corporate audiences, celebrities and the general public through specialty programming events as well as conversations amongst the Foundation's social media platforms. These objectives were then broken down into measurable strategies and specific tactics that all tied together. Each strategy and tactic is to be evaluated and measured by the client using a three-tier scale created specifically for this campaign to decipher if the overall objectives were met. Due to time constraints, the team was unfortunately unable to complete everything they wanted to, so they created a list of recommendations for the client that could potentially be implemented in future Irie Foundation campaigns.

Finally, the Irie Foundation Special Events team worked on creating the binder for the client by compiling all the campaign materials in addition to the all-encompassing appendices with all other related materials. The appendices include all the data from both the primary and secondary research, as well writing tactical pieces, social media posts, design samples and more. Lastly, the entire PowerPoint presentation for the client is included at the end of the binder as an overview of the campaign.

Irie Foundation and Irie Weekend: Issue Statement

The primary issues facing Irie Weekend and Irie Foundation stem from a lack of connectivity between the Weekend and Foundation itself, resulting in an absence of awareness around the Foundation's efforts and an inadequate pre-promotion strategy that fails to focus the target audience on those benefiting from the Foundation.

Irie Foundation Special Events: Situation Analysis and SWOT for Irie Foundation

<u>Client Background</u>

Irie Foundation is a registered 501(c)(3) organization working to create positive impacts for South Florida's at-risk youth. The Foundation seeks to inspire students from middle school onward to pursue higher education, assisting them on their journey toward becoming successful adults. The mission statement of the Foundation is:

> *Irie Foundation seeks to empower South Florida's at-risk youth to lead productive lives through mentorship programs, cultural experiences and scholarship opportunities. By following the young people, it serves from middle school through high school, the Foundation's ultimate goal is to inspire and encourage its students to graduate high school, pursue higher education and develop into successful adults.*

Irie Foundation was first established in 2011. The idea came from DJ Irie, a Miami-based DJ and philanthropist, who would volunteer for other organizations throughout South Florida. While volunteering, DJ Irie was exposed to these charities consistently fulfilling their initiatives and giving back to the community, inspiring him to set out and do the same. As a result, DJ Irie created Irie Foundation. Irie Foundation was molded after the things DJ Irie was most passionate about; music and children.

In partnership with the Carnival Foundation, Miami Heat Charitable Fund and Big Brothers Big Sisters of Greater Miami, Irie Foundation has created a new state-of-the-art education center for Foundation programming. Irie Rhythms Academy is located on the fourth floor of the new Carnival for Excellence Building, located at 550 LeJune Road in Miami. Participants of the Foundation now have free access to music, arts and literacy programs, all of which fall under the Foundation's STEAM curriculum. The academy serves as a multipurpose space; offering services for professionals in the music and technology sectors. Some of the projected programs include; DJ events, recording and mixing classes, audio and visual photography, vocal lessons and instrumental lessons. This new facility also houses a brand-new computer lab, a fully stocked library, comfortable space for homework or tutoring, a recording studio and a fitness room donated by the Miami Heat Charitable Fund.

<u>Internal Audit/Assesment</u>

Irie Foundation has several staff members that work together, making Irie Foundation's vision a reality. These staff members include:
- DJ Irie, *Founder*
- Shobhna Callaghan, *Managing Director for Irie Group of Companies*
- Kyle Post, *Director of Operations and Programs for Irie Foundation*
- Felicia Quanning, *Director of Public Relations for Irie Group of Companies*
- Johnae Mann, *Operations and Public Relations Administrator for Irie Foundation*
- Ashley Buncik, *Client Services Manager for Irie Music Group*

DJ Irie is a sought-after philanthropist, entertainer and entrepreneur with a larger than life personality. He has served as the official DJ of the NBA's Miami Heat, Carnival Cruise Lines and superstar Jamie Foxx. Additionally, he has been a brand ambassador to Heineken, New Era, Premier Beverage and Verizon Wireless. He has won numerous awards such as the Charles E. Perry Young Alumni Visionary of the Year, Global Spin Awards' Club DJ of the Year and has been featured on a multitude of television talk shows. Along with his stardom, DJ Irie is a continuous supporter of many local and national non-profit organizations. DJ Irie is heavily involved with the Foundation and continues to work with his team to expand upon it as years progress.

Shobhna Callaghan, is the glue that holds the business function together. She governs the organization's support services; including finance, human resources and legal. She is responsible for building and maintaining an effective team and assumes full accountability for Irie Group's operations. She continually works to ensure that the strategic direction of the organization is maintained, working to increase the effectiveness of the Irie Group of Companies overall.

Kyle Post is responsible for the operational success of the Foundation. He ensures seamless team management across the Foundation and spearheads the activations of Irie Foundation's programs. Additionally, he is the external face of the Foundation to the community and is the only team member listed on Irie Foundation's website, besides founder DJ Irie. Kyle joined Irie Foundation in January 2015 and offers a unique wealth of experience from his experience as a performer and entertainment programmer for Walt Disney World and Carnival Cruise Lines. As a project manager, Kyle has successfully piloted several municipal and multi-national youth-centric community development initiatives in partnership with A Spring of Hope, JetBlue Airways Corporation, KaBOOM! and South African Airways. His strategic leadership in improving internal and external communication, creating rapid organizational growth and fostering ongoing operational sustainability has catapulted Irie Foundation into the top tier of national service organizations.

Felicia Quanning, Director of Public Relations for Irie Group of Companies, is tasked with managing and facilitating the company's day-to-day communications activities. She works to administer press relations, seek out new media platforms and provides communications counsel to senior management. She is also responsible for developing and executing long-term communications strategies that align with the business's vision and direction.

Johnae Mann supports the implementation of overall operations strategies that serve to enhance the quality, efficiency and market development of new and existing partnerships for Irie Foundation. She manages the strategic communications activities that promote, enhance and protect the company's brand reputation. Additionally, she serves as the official spokesperson for the company.

Ashley Buncik, Irie Music Group's Client Services Manager, is the primary contact for brand's partnerships. Her primary responsibilities include everything from identifying opportunities that increase brand exposure to ensuring that deliverables are met. She is consistently communicating with clients, partners and sponsors, aiming to achieve the highest level of client satisfaction possible.

In order to attain the Foundation's goals, they have partnered with several organizations. The current sponsors for Irie Foundation are: After-School All-Stars South Florida, Big Brothers Big Sisters of Greater Miami and South Dade Toyota. Irie Foundation is also sponsored by several entities including Carnival Foundation, Ford, JetBlue, Jimmy Johns, the Miami Heat and more.

Irie Foundation offers numerous programs for underserved and at-risk youth from Miami-Dade County, working to enlighten these children with sociocultural experiences that would otherwise be unavailable to them. Irie Foundation's Cultural Passport Program offers different "activations" for Foundation participants, ranging from performing and fine arts to sporting events and more. These activations are currently offered at least once a month from September to June. The Foundation also recognizes high school seniors who have overcome adversity in achieving graduation and college acceptances at its annual collaboration with Big Brothers Big Sisters. At this ceremony, students are awarded with the Impact Scholarship Fund for their journey toward higher education. The Impact Scholarship Fund is inclusive of the Impact Scholarship for academic merit, the Theresa "Boogie" Grocher Scholarship for outstanding community service and the Road to Success Car Giveaway for dedication of achievement. As of September 2017, Irie Foundation has presented 14 graduating seniors with Impact Scholarships totaling more than $99,000 and the Foundation's Driving Your Success initiative has awarded two cars courtesy of South Dade Toyota to two deserving graduates. Lastly, Irie Foundation has a My Life Mentoring program presented by Jimmy John's where different mentors come in-person to talk to students, encouraging them to stay in school and improve their grades. These goals are achieved by providing children with the ability to meet influential people who can serve as mentors for them.

Public Perception

Irie Foundation heavily relies on three forms of social media to communicate with members of their target audience; Instagram, Twitter and Facebook. Its username handle, "@iriefoundaiton" is the same for each of these platforms, creating a consistent image for the organization.

Irie Foundation's Facebook page has 1,299 likes and 1,289 followers. The Facebook page has only been reviewed by three people, however all three of them gave Irie Foundation five out of five stars. There is little interaction on Irie Foundation's posts, however people that do choose to interact primarily use positive verbiage, congratulating the Foundation on its accomplishments and thanking volunteers as well as team members for their work. *(See below for samples of interaction on Irie Foundation's posts.)*

Visitor posts about Irie Foundation are also positive, but scarce. The posts are primarily curated by partners, sponsors and members of Irie Foundation. The posts consist of thanking the Foundation for their work with the community, promoting an upcoming Foundation event or congratulating the Foundation on a job well done following an event; all of which paint Irie Foundation in a positive light.

Irie Foundation's Instagram platform has 3,069 followers. Their social media posts get around 90 likes per post and an average of one to three comments on each. These comments are primarily positive, portraying a positive public perception toward Irie Foundation. Majority of the comments are commemorating the Foundation on their cause and asking how to get further involved in the Foundation itself. *(See below for samples of interaction on Irie Foundation's posts.)*

The Foundation's Twitter account has 1,591 followers and is following 1,195 people. They have tweeted 2,698 times, but usually get less than 10 favorites for most of its posts. There is not much conversation from the public on this platform, however followers are retweeting Irie Foundation's posts proving that they agree with or like the content Irie Foundation is putting out. From these retweets, one can infer that this audience has a neutral to positive view of Irie Foundation.

Furthermore, the media tends to cover the celebrities present at the Weekend's events as opposed to diving into the true cause behind the Weekend's activities. All except one article failed to connect the purpose of Irie Weekend back to Irie Foundation.

External Audit/Assessment

There are many external forces that impact and influence Irie Foundation. One of these major forces is competition with other after-school programs, from elementary school to high school, due to their convenience. Schools in Miami-Dade County offer after-school programs and extracurricular activities that help entertain and keep children off the streets. Since majority these programs are held on the school's campus, parents don't have to worry about transporting their children elsewhere. Furthermore, parents whose children are the target market for Irie Foundation may not have the economic means to transport their children to and from Irie Rhythms Academy. This could create competition between Irie Foundation and current after-school programs, as there is no transportation available for children to and from the new building.

Additionally, Miami-Dade is a highly-saturated area in terms of philanthropic organizations. Although people in the area might be affluent, there are so many options as to where they can donate their money. Therefore, people in the area tend to spread their money thin and donate small amounts to several causes as opposed to big amounts to one cause. A lack of sustainable donations and help can affect Irie Rhythms Academy, as it operates based on money from donations and fundraisers.

The next external force impacting Irie Foundation is the opening and dedication of the new Irie Rhythms Academy building being consistently delayed. Due to this, the expansion of Irie Foundation's programming for underserved youth has also been delayed. Additionally, this setback has taken away the Foundation's extra source of income, as Irie Rhythms Academy plans to rent out the recording studio, but cannot do this until the center is officially open. During this delayed time, the Foundation is unable to offer its state-of-the-art education and technology center to children, helping them stay out of harm's way and off the streets.

Another external threat is inclimate weather, which is not uncommon in South Florida. Irie Foundation events and programming are heavily reliant on good weather and being outside, as an abundance of the Foundation's activities deal with outdoor sports or games. However, due to Miami's unpredictable weather conditions, the Foundation cannot be reliant on hosting these activities outside. Being outdoors during inclimate weather could cause children to become sick, result in injuries or produce overall discomfort. The weather heavily influences Irie Foundation's capabilities and therefore the Foundation must have a back-up plan to avoid being put in this situation.

Lastly, while working with children, there is always the external factor of safety. Irie Foundation must be consciousness of accidents that may arise during programming or while having children showcase their talents at Irie Weekend. These accidents could span anywhere from food allergies, to health outbreaks, to injuries that may occur under Irie Foundation's care and more. These accidents may be amplified with the increasing number of participants in the program, as well as the heightened amount of new activities and programming these children can participate in.

SWOT Analysis

Strengths

- Irie Foundation has loyal partners and sponsors that are looking to give back and support the Foundation.
- Irie Foundation has strong celebrity engagement that can be utilized for both programming and fundraising events.
- Irie Foundation has 13 plus years of experience.
- The Foundation has grown exponentially since 2011.
- Irie Foundation's staff are all very passionate about the organization's cause.
- Miami-Dade County, the county in which Irie Foundation is located, is known for being affluent and generous when it comes to donations.
- DJ Irie has an extensive personal network of celebrities, sponsors and partners that the Foundation can utilize.
- DJ Irie is a public figure, giving Irie Foundation an easier "in" with the media as the founder alone is already newsworthy.

Weaknesses

- There is a prevalent lack of connection between Irie Foundation and Irie Weekend when it comes to outreach.
- Irie Foundation puts out inconsistent messaging around its mission, goals, what the Foundation wants to name things publicly and more.
- Irie Foundation has no strategic timeline in place leading up to Irie Weekend.
- Irie Foundation struggles keeping children active within the organization once they have graduated; losing opportunities for volunteers and mentors.
- Irie Foundation's Irie Rhythms Academy is three to six months behind schedule.
- There are different logos and branding between the Foundation and Irie Weekend.
- There is no fixed, organized budget set aside for special event programming.

Opportunities

- Irie Foundation has celebrities, partners and sponsors capable of assisting with the new opening of Irie Rhythms Academy.
- Irie Foundation can engage local colleges and community members to assist with or teach new programming within the Irie Rhythms Academy.
- Irie Foundation can garner media and news coverage for the opening of its Irie Rhythms Academy, new programs Irie Foundation is offering and more; leading to increased awareness around Irie Foundation overall.

- Irie Foundation can increase social media contests, posts, engagement, interactivity and conversations surrounding the Foundation using DJ Irie's extensive personal network, leading to better interactions as well as greater awareness.
- Irie Foundation can pitch more stories surrounding the Foundation and special events to the media in order to increase interest and awareness.
- Irie Rhythms Academy allows Irie Foundation to expand upon its existing programming, extend its hours of operation and include special event programming.
- Irie Rhythms Academy provides Irie Foundation with an additional source of income that can be used to increase programming for the Foundation itself.

Threats

- Irie Foundation was founded in a highly saturated philanthropic market with many different organizations for South Floridians to donate their money to; resulting in increased competition for Irie Foundation.
- People may choose to not participate or donate to Irie Foundation due to lack of interest and attitudinal problems at the community level.
- The celebrities that engage with Irie Foundation's activities are not fully aware of the mission behind Irie Foundation.
- Other after-school programs in Miami-Dade County serve as competition for Irie Foundation, offering similar programs geared toward the same primary audience.
- Other recording studios in Miami-Dade County could detract from Irie Rhythm Academy's additional source of income, intended to fund more programming opportunities for Irie Foundation.

Irie Foundation Special Events: Audience Research

Primary Audience

The primary audience for Irie Foundation is Generation Z, those born between 1996 to current day, as well as Generation X, those born between 1964 and 1984 and early members of Generation Y that were born in 1985.

Generation Z is a primary audience member for Irie Foundation because it is the main demographic the organization caters its programming toward. Irie Foundation focuses majority of its efforts on helping underserved, at-risk youth from this demographic in Miami-Dade County, specifically those in public schools from late elementary school to high school. The Foundation does not target Gen-Zers younger than fifth grade as the Foundation currently only provides programming for middle school and high school students. Gen Z is the reason Irie Foundation was founded, and the core recipient of the Foundation's efforts.

Generation X is also a primary audience member for Irie Foundation. This audience is made up of parents in Miami-Dade County who enroll their children in Irie Foundation programming and events. Irie Foundation must cater to this audience so that they continue to support their children's involvement in the Foundation. Gen X-ers also serve as a great source of volunteers and donors for the Foundation to target.

Early members of Generation Y make up the last portion of Irie Foundation's primary audience. This audience consists of parents in Miami-Dade County, who most likely have children aged 10-11 that are in fifth grade. These parents must be targeted by Irie Foundation to raise their awareness of what the Foundation has to offer, making these parents more likely to sign their children up to participate in Foundation programming and events from middle school onward. This target audience also serves as a great source of volunteers and donors for the Foundation.

Secondary Audience

The secondary audience for Irie Foundation is Baby Boomers, those born between 1946 and 1963, that serve as the grandparents of Gen Z-ers. Additionally, Generation Y, those born between 1985 and 1995, are another secondary audience as they're members of the community that could volunteer or donate to Irie Foundation.

Baby Boomers in Miami-Dade County serve as a secondary audience member for Irie Foundation because they are the grandparents of Gen Z, the underserved youth with which Irie Foundation programming and events were created to serve. Majority of these Boomers are older and have money saved up for retirement. Therefore, what better way to spend this money than by donating it to a cause in which their grandchildren are a part of. Boomers must be targeted by Irie Foundation as a source of donations and income to keep the Foundation running for Gen Z in the community.

Generation Y, or Millennials, in Miami-Dade County are also a secondary audience member for Irie Foundation as they make up the surrounding community. Millennials should be targeted by Irie Foundation for their donations and ability to volunteer. Many

Millennials are looking for a way to give back to their community and help charitable causes, but don't know how to get involved or which organization to choose.

Generation Z

Gen Z is 60 million-strong, consisting of people between the ages of 21-years-old to present. Gen Z is one of the only generations born entirely in the internet era, and they have parents that are generally more accepting of knowledge and technology. By the age of 4 or 5, majority of Gen Z has ditched traditional toys such as Barbies and toy cars, opting for computers, cell phones and video games as their primary source of entertainment. This generation does not remember a world without cell phones or the latest technology, therefore they are heavily reliant on these tools and prioritize them in their daily lives.

Due to their large consumption of technology and consistent exposure to advertisements, Gen Z tends to be savvy consumers who know what they want and how to get it. Gen Z are overly saturated with brands, with 61 percent of children aged eight to 17 having TV's in their rooms, and are very particular on where they choose to purchase from. Television is the main way this generation is exposed to big brands. Statistics show that 75 percent of 6-8 year olds and 56 percent of 9-11 year olds ask their parents to buy things they see in commercials on television. Gen Z has grown up in an era where information is readily available to them always, therefore they are not trusting of brands and have a tendency of rejecting big companies. Gen Z also tends to trust individuals more than large institutions. As a result, many brands are starting to partner with social media influencers to get their brand names out there and appear more relatable to Gen Z-ers. Gen Z also resonates better with images, symbols and emoticons as opposed to lengthy amounts of text. Therefore, brands are learning to communicate with Gen Z-ers in this preferred manner. The way to market products and services to this generation is in ways that emphasize acceptance from their peers and society.

A survey by Lincoln Financial Group revealed that members of Gen Z are saving earlier and more than any other generation when it comes to spending. Out of 400 Gen Z-ers aged 15 to 19, 60 percent claimed to already have savings accounts set up and 71 percent said they are focused on saving for their future. When Gen Z isn't saving their money, they prioritize finding the best value for their money when making a purchase. This generation has a spending power of more than $44 billion in the U.S. alone.

Lastly, Gen Z-ers are very competitive and independent. They have grown up with their parents teaching them that there is a grave distinction between winners and losers in this world, and that they should want to be on the winning team. They are an accepting generation, of both political matters and social matters, and are not as judgmental as other generations.

<u>Prepackaged Audiences for Generation Z</u>

Students in the Miami-Dade Public School System
Irie Foundation targets underserved students from late elementary school to high school in the Miami-Dade Public School System. This system is the fourth largest school district in the United States, comprised of more than 345,000 students. Students in the Miami-Dade Public School System are the main beneficiaries of Irie Foundation's programs, coming from all different communities ranging from rural and suburban to urban cities and municipalities. Therefore, students are extremely diverse, as seen through the 56 different languages and 160 countries represented in the district.

Elementary school students in Miami-Dade Public School System
Irie Foundation must target underserved elementary school students between the ages of 10 and 11, that are primarily in fifth grade in the Miami-Dade Area. These students are going to graduate and then have the opportunity to play an active role within Irie Foundation. The Foundation must start advertising and garnering the attention of these students to assure that they are aware of this opportunity and to get them excited about participating.

Middle school students in Miami-Dade Public School System
In the Miami-Dade Public Schools System, middle schools include grades six, seven and eight. Irie Foundation must target underserved middle school students, aged 10 to 14, that are enrolled in public schools throughout Miami-Dade County. Middle school students fall in the middle age range of Gen Z. These students are in that in-between stage, or that 'awkward middle school stage' and are easily influenced and affected by others. Therefore, Irie Foundation serves as a positive influencer in these children's lives, giving them a safe, controlled environment and keeping them off the streets at a time where they could easily experiment with the wrong group of people or with the wrong things.

High school students in Miami-Dade Public School System
In the Miami-Dade Public Schools System, high schools include grades nine, 10, 11 and 12. Irie Foundation must target underserved high school students, aged 14 to 18, that are enrolled in public schools throughout Miami-Dade County. As mentioned above, Gen Z-ers at this age primarily have savings accounts and are already focusing on their futures. Individuals at this age are highly vulnerable as they attempt to figure out plans post-graduation and attempt to find themselves as they're given more responsibility and the 'social scene' seems like a high priority to one's success. Therefore, Irie Foundation is important in allowing these individuals to learn and grow in a safe environment that helps them discover who they are.

<u>Generation X</u>

Generation X is an estimated 50 million-strong, consisting of those between the ages of 33 and 53 years old. Gen X is highly educated and sophisticated, with more than 60 percent of the population having attained a degree in higher education.

During the beginning stages of this generation in the 1960's, early Gen X-ers witnessed their parents becoming more hands off and lenient in their parenting style. Divorce rates increased during this time and fertility rates plummeted. Therefore, Gen X-ers learned young how to be resilient and fend for themselves. They entered a job market with a buoyant economy and as a result, embraced the high-turnover, no-safety net lifestyle. This generation suffered the most in the Great Recession, with many struggling to keep their homes and provide for their families. In an era where steady employment was hard to find, many Gen X-ers chose to prioritize time with their families over long work hours. They prefer temporary jobs over full-time positions and hope to build better relationships with their families than their parents did with them.

Gen X-ers are very heavily connected to the generation below them and above them. According to the Pew Research Center, 47 percent of adults in their 40's and 50's have a parent aged 65 or older and are either raising a young child or financially supporting a grown child. Additionally, approximately 15 percent of these adults are providing financial support to an aging parent and a child. Gen-Xers are in the position to take over jobs, companies and politics of the generation before them, placing them in a position of high influence.

Gen X also has an ample amount of spending power. This generation has 29 percent of the U.S.'s total estimated net worth dollars and 31 percent of the total income dollars. When purchasing items, Gen X does not respond well to generic marketing approaches. They like to be very well informed prior to making a purchase decision and most won't consider buying a product until they've read the online reviews or social media opinions. Gen X-ers prefer when retailers provide personalized brand experiences for them and like when marketing messages are straight-forward and truthful. Additionally, Gen Xers are digitally driven, with 60 percent of them using their cellphones daily, 67 percent of them using their laptops daily and 75 percent of them using social media at least once a month. When it comes to generation preference, Gen X-ers relate best to warm, earthy colors that remind them of nature as well as the sleek, modern, industrial look. This is important for advertisers trying to target this generation.

In terms of communication, targeting Gen X-ers is not an easy task. Traditional network TV is not an effective way to target this generation, especially Gen X-er men. They have a lack of respect for modern forms of advertising and prefer informal communication styles. Gen X-ers prefer having access to information and being educated before buying. They also value straightforward facts, honesty and candor. Marketers should ask them for feedback and share information with them regularly to target them effectively. In other words, act more as their consultant instead of a seller. Gen X-ers tend to think communally so group events and word-of-mouth recommendations from their peers are effective ways of marketing for them. The most effective methods of communication for this generation are the internet, email, multi-media, direct mail, word-of-mouth, social events and peer gatherings.
Gen X-ers value sincerity, authenticity and independence. They adapt well to change and are tolerant of alternative lifestyles. Gen X-ers are ambitious and eager to learn new things, but they like to take things at their own pace and accomplish things on their own.

Prepackaged Audiences for Generation X

Low-Income Parents with Students in the Miami-Dade Public School System
Parents with low-incomes in Miami-Dade County that send their children to school in the Miami-Dade Public School System are a pre-packaged target audience for Irie

Foundation. This group of parents tend to have lower paying jobs and work longer hours. Therefore, they most likely do not have time to pick their children up from school, pay for an after-school service or hire a nanny. Irie Foundation must focus on this audience as the Foundation offers a free-service for these parents to utilize, keeping their children off the streets and giving them a positive environment to learn in.

Philanthropic Donors
According to research conducted by Advancement Resources, Generation X wants to engage in philanthropies as well as know that these philanthropies are making a difference. Therefore, middle to upper-class Gen-Xers within Miami-Dade County that follow this practice of wanting to give back, serve as a perfect target, as Irie Foundation is giving back to underserved youth within these Gen-Xer's neighborhoods. They will directly see the difference their contribution is making and therefore, will choose to donate both time and money to the Foundation to make a difference.

Attendees of Irie Weekend
Gen-Xers that previously attended Irie Weekend are a pre-packaged audience as they have attended Irie Foundation's primary philanthropic event, establishing a connection to the cause. These Gen-Xers are middle to upper-class individuals within Miami-Dade County that know about the Foundation and have prioritized giving back in the past; making them a great audience to target for future donations and volunteerism.

Irie Foundation Special Events: Secondary Research Summary

<u>Introduction</u>

Through secondary research, the teams gathered information on nonprofit organizations, marketing and communication strategies for nonprofits, nonprofit programming and special events, and competitors of the Irie Foundation. Summaries of this research have been broken down into categories title nonprofit organizations, public relations for nonprofits, nonprofit programming, special events for nonprofit organizations, and competition summary. The information in this summary should be regarded as a basis for legitimizing the effectiveness of the proposed plan.

<u>Nonprofit Organizations</u>

According to the article "Understanding public awareness of nonprofit organizations: exploring the awareness–confidence relationship" by Lindsey McDougle (2014), nonprofits are believed to have the organizational scope and connections to local communities necessary to deliver effective social services in cost-effective ways. Nonprofit organizations are an integral part of our communities, providing a vast array of services, fostering civic participation and building social cohesion (Lassiter, 2007). However, a majority of the public is unaware of nonprofits' services in their community, and therefore are unable to find, volunteer at or donate to these organizations (McDougle, 2014).

Dr. Brooke Weberling McKeever in "From Awareness to Advocacy: Understanding Nonprofit Communication, Participation, and Support" (2013) highlights that public support and awareness toward nonprofit organizations is primarily driven by problem and constraint recognition, personal involvement, behavior intentions and subjective norms. Public confidence in nonprofits is also a critical indicator of awareness, and can be influenced or changed by individual characteristics associated with nonprofit awareness (McDougle, 2014).

Current Awareness
A survey of public attitudes toward nonprofit organizations found that racial and ethnic minorities, people with lower incomes and individuals not registered to vote had greater difficulty identifying nonprofits in their community; raising concerns for organizations catered specifically toward these individuals (McDougle, 2014). In fact, those who contribute the most to nonprofit organizations are the most aware of what these nonprofits stand for and their values, as opposed to those who do not contribute and suffer from lack of these services (Havens, O'Herlihy, & Schervish, 2006).

The number of nonprofit donations and volunteers vastly increases as organizational awareness increases, with a study showing that individuals who demonstrated higher levels of nonprofit awareness were two-to-three times more likely to show greater levels of confidence in these organizations (McDougle, 2014). Confidence levels can be greatly increased by the act of actively giving to organizations (Light, 2004). A study conducted after 9/11 shows a spike in giving directed toward nonprofit organizations and as a result, a 19 percent increase in public confidence toward these nonprofits (Light, 2004).

Currently, individuals with a college degree or higher are nearly four times as likely to have greater nonprofit awareness than those without (McDougle, 2014). Another study conducted in 2002 reveals that 55 percent of respondents with a high school education or less claim to have a 'fair amount' of confidence in nonprofits, compared to the 68 percent of college-educated respondents saying they have a 'great amount' of confidence in nonprofits (Light, 2004). College-educated, high-income Americans prove to be more confident than their peers surrounding nonprofit awareness (Light, 2004).

Additionally, Caucasian individuals tend to have higher levels of awareness than other ethnicities, and people with higher income levels are 16 percent more likely to have greater nonprofit awareness (McDougle, 2014). Religion also comes into play when examining nonprofit awareness, as those who self-identify with some form of religious practice are more likely to show greater confidence in nonprofits and obtain greater awareness (McDougle, 2014). Religious causes are, and always have been, Americans' favorite charitable targets and those who support houses of worship and clergy to maintain the faith are more likely to donate than those who identify as non-religious (Light, 2004).

Perceived Constraints

Perceived constraints, such as limited time and money, are big obstacles in terms of hindering nonprofit awareness for an upcoming event (McKeever, 2013). Regardless of how people may feel about the cause, organization, or event, these constraints are the dominant reason one may choose not to participate or give back to a nonprofit organization (McKeever, 2013). For an organization to be efficient and effective, it must develop organizational commitment and energy to facilitate continued process improvement by decreasing negative stigmas surrounding it (Lassiter, 2007). Decreasing these constraints through actions such as lessening the cost of an event, or designing external messaging that addresses and minimizes these constraints, may help to overcome this obstacle and increase participation in nonprofit organizations (McKeever, 2013). Decreasing the negativities around nonprofits, specifically the hassle of giving money or asking friends and family members for monetary donations, also leads to increased participation and awareness for nonprofits (McKeever, 2013). Nonprofits rely heavily on charitable donations, but when addressing the community, "Charitable Giving: How Much, By Whom, To What, and How?" published in "The Nonprofit Sector: A Research Handbook" by John J. Havens, Mary A. O'Herlihy and Paul G. Schervish (2006) suggests paying close attention to average contribution rates—male's giving $1,858 yearly and women giving $1,594 yearly for contributing households—and specifically targeting those with a history of giving back to assure nonprofits get the most value for their time and do not aggravate those whom are unfit to give back.

Subjective Norms

Personal involvements or connections to a nonprofit adds to one's information gaining, one's willingness to learn more about a specific organization and get involved, yet these personal connections do not predict behavioral intentions when it comes to participation in nonprofit events (McKeever, 2013). Giving to an organization creates an intense connection to its efforts, which helps to explain increased confidence, ultimately leading to increased support and a higher chance of participation from individuals (Light, 2004). One's readiness to participate in a nonprofit or give back can however be influenced by increasing positive subjective norms and social expectations, such as reiterating why participating in nonprofits is a good thing and making one feel as if they'd be the odd one out if they were to not participate (McKeever, 2013). The bottom line is that nonprofit organizations do little to boost civic involvement as they satisfy this need for involvement by imposing significant personal costs, that may actually discourage direct participation (Havens, O'Herlihy & Schervish, 2006). Therefore, nonprofits must change their strategy, redirecting civic involvement into a positive (Havens, O'Herlihy & Schervish, 2006).

Past Participation

Past participation in an organization or event is also a leading factor that increases nonprofit volunteers and overall organizational awareness, yet year-over-year participation is dependent on whether or not the individual organization places an emphasis on volunteer retention—keeping volunteers happy while they work so they'll want to participate again in the future (McKeever, 2013). Participation is often sustained by positive interactions with significant others, especially friends and family members (Havens, O'Herlihy & Schervish, 2006). To sustain mass participation, organizations must maintain concrete programs with specific goals (Havens, O'Herlihy & Schervish, 2006).

Overall, it is evident that public awareness toward nonprofit organizations is critical for garnering support, increasing donations, maintaining volunteers and spreading positive word of mouth on the community level, assuring that intended recipients of such nonprofits successfully receive foundational efforts in an effective way.

Public Relations for Nonprofits

Public Relations is the set of activities involved in reaching the attention and or interest of media outlets (Harrison, 2013). The goal of Public Relation practitioners is to maximize positive coverage through mass media publicity without having to pay to advertise (Harrison, 2013). Thus, what makes mass media publicity a more trustworthy option is that you don't – and can't – pay for it, therefore you can't "control" it (Beckwith, 2005). In the article "*Publicity for Nonprofits*" author Sandra Beckwith (2005) states that although controlled advertising and direct mail campaigns should have a place in nonprofits marketing plan, neither marketing effort has the impact that free range exposure has. Another advantage, is its high credibility as oppose to paid advertising due to third party endorsements (Harrison, 2013). "The credibility-building role of publicity helps your organization to strengthen its customer and employee relationship" (Harrison, 2013). Therefore, "Public relations should be a top priority for your nonprofit organization, as the more positive an image your organization is creating, the more opportunities you will find to accomplish your mission and goals" (Priutt, 2016).

"While many consider the media a fearsome adversary, it can be a powerful ally if approached strategically" (Weinreich, 2006). Publicity makes something or someone known (Harrison, 2013). "The media sells their audiences to their advertisers and program sponsors as potential buyers of their products and services" (Harrison, 2013). If done well, you can reach large numbers of people in your target audience and, with a carefully crafted message, influence their ideas and opinions (Weinreich, 2006).

The key to success is merely based on the things you do behind the scenes to control and shape the message you are presenting to the media (Beckwith, 2005). "It is crucial to set PR objectives that are realistic for your nonprofit and, make sure your organization knows what results it wants out of the campaign" (Priutt, 2016). According to the article "*Your Media Relations Should Have a Strategic Purpose*" by Kim Harrison (2013) the best practice public relations activity involves a clear and strategic connection to your organizational mission and goals. Understanding these, shapes whom you want to reach with your message and which media outlets you want to target (Weinreich, 2006).

Beckwith (2005) says that "a basic tenet of publicity is that your information has to be newsworthy." Since the media gatekeepers have their own criteria for judging what is worth covering, you will need to frame the issue in an appeling way to get their attention (Weinreich, 2006). A trick to get the desired coverage is to learn how to think like the media or editor you will be contacting (Beckwith, 2005). Another thing Beckwith (2005) recommends is to study your target media outlet, "it will make you a better 'pitcher'". Media representatives are known to be more receptive to pitches from people who are familiar with what they do and the things they have produced in the past (Beckwith, 2005). Start to establish beneficial relationships before you pitch them the story, give them reactions to their stories and provide them with an information packet on your organization for future reference (Weinreich, 2006). "Your media strategies should be chosen wisely to help your nonprofit reach a specified communication objective for your target audiences" (Priutt, 2016).

Once you have identified your media target audience, the next step is to mold your message – combine what you have learned about your target and brainstorm possible persuasive messages (Beckwith, 2005). The information presented must be solid, easy and attractive, in order to shape the interpretations and opinions of what people are learning about your organization (Harrison, 2013). In the article, "*The DOs and DON'Ts of Public Relation Strategies for Nonprofits,*" author Ronald Priutt (2016) supports this by saying that, every organization must define its unique story and let communities know the value they are providing. "This story should be built on defined messages that clearly position and differentiate the organization" (Priutt, 2016). Think about what you want people to do; what kind of action do you want them to take, Donate? Volunteers? Attend an event? Support a cause? (Beckwith, 2005).

Reference List

Apsler, R. (2009). After-school programs for adolescents: A review of evaluation research. *Adolescence, 44*(173), 1-19.

Beckwith, S. L. (January, 2005). *Publicity for nonprofit: generating media exposure that leads to awareness, growth, and contributions* 57-81.

Bramwell, B. (1997). Strategic planning before and after a mega-event. *Tourism Management, 18*(3), 167-176.

Clardy, B. (2007). *Making the Most of Your Special Event.* Arlington, VA: Association of Fundraising Professionals.

Diversi, M., & Mecham, C. (2004). Latino(a) students and Caucasian mentors in a rural after-school program: Towards empowering adult-youth relationships. *Journal of Community Psychology, 33*(1), 31-40. doi:10.1002/jcop.20034

Duerden, M. D., & Gillard, A. (2011). An approach to theory-based youth programming. *New Directions for Youth Development, 2011*(S1), 39-53. doi:10.1002/yd.418

Education & Youth Development. (2014). Retrieved October 28, 2017, from https://nonprofits.miamifoundation.org/categories/education-youth-development

Enache, I., & Zdeněk, B. (2011). Student Behavior and Student Satisfaction – A Marketing Approach. *Scientific Papers of the University of Pardubice*, 48-52. Retrieved from https://dk.upce.cz/handle/10195/42500

Evans, R. (1995). Special events: Where is institutional integrity? *Fund Raising Management, 26*(5), 26.

Harrison, K. (August, 2013). *Your media relations should have a strategic purpose. Cutting Edge PR.* 2005 – 2013 Cutting Edge PR.

Havens, J. J., O'Herlihy, M. A., & Schervish, P. G. (2006). *The nonprofit sector: a research handbook* (W. W. Powell & R. Steinberg, Eds.). New Haven: Yale University Pres.

Hawthorne, R. (n.d.). *Five Ways to Build Your Nonprofit Brand's Buzzability* . Retrieved September 3, 2017, from nonprofithub.org: http://nonprofithub.org/nonprofit-branding/five-ways-build-nonprofit-brands-buzzability/

Kalivretenos, A. (2015). The Importance of Music Education. Retrieved September 24, 2017, from https://thehumanist.com/features/articles/the-importance-of-music-education

Irie Foundation Special Events: Primary Research

<u>Introduction</u>

Secondary Research Summary

The Foundation Teams' secondary research reported on several concepts relevant to nonprofit organizations and specific to Irie Foundation, including increasing awareness and effective programming strategies, as well as an analysis of potential competitors to Irie Foundation. Firstly, it comes as no surprise that nonprofit organizations are seen as integral to our communities in terms of providing services, fostering civic participation and building social cohesion. However, a majority of the public is found to be unaware of nonprofit services in their community, which leads to an inability to find, volunteer or donate to these organizations. Donations and volunteers of nonprofit organizations tend to be greatly associated with organizational awareness, which also shows a trend with organizational confidence. Increases in donations of time or funds to nonprofits can result by actively working to lessen the supporter's perceived constraints like limited time and money. Decreasing any negatives surrounding nonprofits, such as many current practices used to collect donations, will also result in increased participation and awareness of nonprofit organizations. Ultimately, public awareness of the organization is critical for gathering support, increasing donations, and maintaining volunteers.

Successfully promoting a nonprofit strengthens the relationship between the organization and its intended audience, meaning the furthering of the organization's goals and mission. One of the largest errors those promoting nonprofits can make is to believe that successfully marketing their organization greatly differs from that of a for-profit company or organization. Regardless of the mission of the organization, the emphasis of the public relations practitioner should be on creating thoughtful content that is engaging to the intended audiences, including both the media and those benefitting as a result of the organization's work. Since many nonprofit organizations have a sharp focus on benefitting the community in which they are operating, and therefore are in competition with other nonprofits, the organization must define its unique story and make its communities aware of the contributions they are making.

When it comes to effective programming for the nonprofit, programs must be a balance of collaborative and specific to a participant's/student's needs. In the case of Irie Foundation, many of the proposed ideas for programming take place after school hours, or during scheduled school recess periods such as summer break. Research suggests that these types of programs are most successful when activities are hands-on and maintain engagement. With the Generation Z students of today, this idea is especially crucial given the considerable difference in the processing of information between themselves and their predecessors.

While programs might be an integral part to the mission of a nonprofit, the case for Irie Foundation, the goals of mostly every nonprofit depend on funding, and a frequent way to secure funds is through special events. Special events have the opportunity to attract more money and greater insight into the mission of a non-profit and, if executed properly, provide a positive experience for all in attendance to associate with the organization. The work of most successful events does not end once the doors close, however. What keeps people coming back to the next large event benefitting a nonprofit is the gratitude shown by the organization and being updated periodically of the impact their contributions or attendance had on the mission and audiences of the organization. The use of social media as a means to engage is very useful here. Combined with a strategic plan and evaluation of promotion and logistics, the event being planned, successful or not, is sure to be improved for the future.

Primary Research Introduction
Conducting primary research enables the Ire Foundation team to fill gaps in knowledge and complete a more comprehensive research report upon which conclusions can be drawn for different strategies, tactics and ideas for this campaign.

Methodology

Introduction
The purpose of secondary research was to explore information previously collected concerning issues and topics applicable to this campaign. After identifying gaps in the secondary research, our teams proceeded to create surveys to be administered to people who fall within the primary audiences of Irie Foundation.

Phase 1: Creation of Primary Research Tool
- Teams determined that in-person interviews would be the most effective method in gathering the type of data needed for adequate support of the objectives strategies.
- Interviews in person would also provide the best setting to be able to ask follow-up questions to a given response.
- Team members drafted questions they determined to be legitimate and necessary to collect the most descriptive and useful information.
- Interviews were recorded and compiled among the two Foundation teams to ensure the most efficient asking of questions.
- Questions were organized to ensure an appropriate sectioning and flow of the interview.

Phase 2: Demographics
- The survey software Qualtrics was to be used to complete the demographics questionnaire. However, given research limitations (discussed later), the demographics questionnaire moved to being a part of the in-person interview.
- The U.S. Census Bureau's terminology was used for questions related to race/ethnicity.
- The demographics questions included:
  - Age
    - Respondents were given the directive to not complete the survey if they were under the age of 18
  - Gender
  - Ethnicity
  - Annual household income (an optional question)

- o Highest completed degree or level of schooling
- o Employment status
- o Children in household
- o Charitable actions
- o Social media use
- o Communication methods
- o Contact preferences
- The types of question used in the demographics questionnaire were:
  - o Multiple choice (single response)
  - o Multiple response
  - o Open-ended text entry

Phase 3: Behavior

Following these demographic questions, our team created a set of questions meant to gauge the behavior of those interviewed and determine their opinions and tendencies when it comes to experiences that overlap with the work of Irie Foundation. This set of questions was divided in regards to:

- Irie Foundation Specific
- Volunteerism
- Children Specific

The complete set of questions as well as each full transcript are available in the appendix.

The questions under each section were as follows:

I. Irie Foundation Specific

- Have you ever heard of Irie Weekend?
- Have you ever heard of Irie Foundation?
  - o How did you hear about Irie Foundation? (If applicable)
  - o Do you know how Irie Foundation obtains their funding for programming? (If applicable)
  - o Has your child ever participated in Irie Foundation programs? (If applicable)
  - o If Irie Foundation offered a summer camp for children, would you sign your child up? If no, why not? (If applicable)
  - o If Irie Foundation offered a special event such as a DJ competition, would you sign your child up or let them participate? If no, why not? (If applicable)
  - o Have you ever donated to Irie Foundation (including donating resources, money, time, etc.)? If so, what? (If applicable)
  - o Irie Foundation is a nonprofit organization serving at-risk youth in Miami-Dade County through after school programming, by providing children with state-of-the-art music and technology resources. Now that you know more about the Foundation, is this an organization you would consider becoming involved in, whether it be donating, volunteering, or sending children to participate? If so why? If no, why not? (If applicable)

II. Volunteerism

- When you hear the word "volunteering," what is the first thing that comes to mind?

- How often do you volunteer a month (including donating resources, money, time, etc.)?
- Have you had any positive volunteer experiences in the past? If so, what made them positive?

III. Children Specific
- Does your child currently participate in any after-school programs?
    - Which ones? (If applicable)
    - How did you initially hear about this (these) specific after-school program(s)? (If applicable)
    - What do you like about this (these) specific after-school program(s)? (If applicable)
    - What is one outcome you would like to see from your child's participation in after-school programs? (If applicable)
- What are your thoughts on incorporating performing arts in your child's education? Why?
- What concepts do you believe are most valuable to your child's education outside of the general scholastic school subjects? (i.e. Math, Science, English, History)
    - Would you ever consider letting your child participate in an after-school program in the future? (If applicable)

Phase 4: Beta Testing

After completing a comprehensive draft of both the demographic section and the behavioral section, members of the class Beta Tested the survey. This was used to check for spelling errors, continuity issues, and the overall look of the survey. Adjustments were made and the Beta Test was re-administered. Final adjustments were made prior to administering the survey to eligible participants.

Phase 5: Administration

Once the interview questions were finalized, each team member was assigned to interview 2-3 people within our target demographic who reside in South Florida. This was to be done by going into the community and using personal contacts of people who had no knowledge of our campaign. Foundation team members administered 19 interviews, each interview was approximately 20-30 minutes in length. Responses were transcribed and sent to research division members for data compilation.

Limitations

The administration of this survey faced several limitations. First, the Foundation teams lost approximately two and a half weeks off of our original timeline of collecting research due to school closure because of severe weather. Although the teams still obtained responses, the original timeline would have provided more time for interviews to occur, thus gathering more data. Another limitation was the team's inability to directly access the parents of children who currently participate in Irie Foundation programs to be interviewed. To make up for this, the teams put a strong emphasis on finding people to interview who fit this target demographic, and who would have children that could potentially participate in Irie Foundation programs.

Results

I. Demographics

Gender
Of those surveyed, 89 percent were female and percent were male

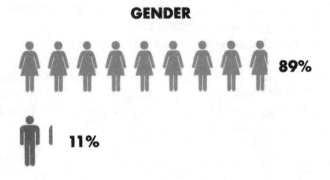

Age
Of those surveyed, 64 percent were members of Generation X, 26 percent were in Generation Y, while 5 percent reside in the Baby Boomer Generation and 5 percent did not report their age.

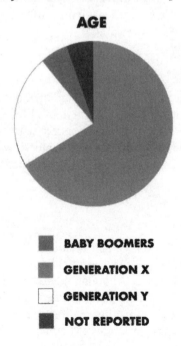

Social Media Use & Communication

When asked about preferred method of communication, 47 percent of respondents said email, 37 percent said text message, 26 percent answered phone call, 21 percent answered social media and 16 percent said mail. Social media use by platform is displayed in the below graph. The percentages represent the percent of respondents who are active on that respective platform.

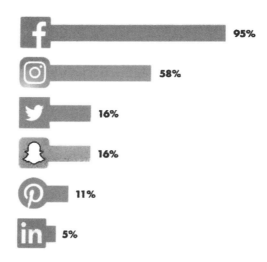

Annual Household Income

An optional question of annual household income was asked as a part of the demographics portion of the interview. While only 37 percent of participants answered this question, the answers ranged from $10,000 to $120,000.

II. Irie Foundation Specific

Only a small portion of those interviewed by Irie Foundation team members had heard of Irie Weekend, while none of the respondents had heard of Irie Foundation. However, after being told more information about the mission of the Foundation, 100 percent of those interviewed said Irie Foundation is an organization they would consider becoming involved in, whether it is donating, volunteering or sending children to participate in.

III. Volunteerism

Approximately 68 percent of those interviewed volunteer (donate time, money, skills, etc.) at least once per month. On the question of what made past volunteer experiences positive, three themes could be determined among the responses:

    1) people have positive volunteer experiences when they are involved in organizations with missions that align with what they are passionate about

2) seeing or receiving first-hand accounts of the effects of volunteering makes volunteers feel their experience was worthwhile

3) people participating in volunteering that is directly benefitting the community in which they reside leave the experience feeling they have actually made a difference.

IV. Children Specific

Approximately 68 percent of the people interviewed had children that participate in after school programs. These programs include things like sports, programs at the Boys & Girls Club and tutoring or academic courses. Parents interviewed described several benefits of their children participating in these after-school programs including how to work as part of a team while also doing things they enjoy. To gauge the opinions of the types of activities and skills Irie Foundation programming provides, parents interviewed were asked for their thoughts on incorporating performing arts into their child's education. All participants responded that incorporating performing arts into their child's education would be beneficial for their children, some citing studies they have heard that show the positive effects of arts education. Participants were also asked what concepts other than general scholastic school subjects (math, science, English, history) they believe are most valuable to their child's education. While many answered that education in the arts and physical activity are important, a strong emphasis was also put on "soft skills," including emotional intelligence, "street smarts" and an appreciation for culture and creativity.

Interpretations of Results

I. Irie Foundation Specific

The mission of Irie Foundation is one that is perceived as positive, given the amount of respondents who said they would potentially volunteer by way of donating time, money or the like. However, knowledge and awareness of Irie Foundation is most likely lacking among a primary demographic, the parents of potential Irie Foundation students who could benefit through their programs. Given the current scope of the Foundation and how they obtain the students that attend their programs, the reach and knowledge of Irie Foundation have sufficed, but as the opening of Irie Rhythms Academy draws nearer, it is crucial the Foundation increases its awareness in order to achieve its goal of helping as many Miami at-risk youth as possible. Along with the opening of its new space, Irie Foundation could also use this opportunity to increase its programming as a way to expand its reach within the community it is looking to serve.

II. Volunteerism

Those surveyed had a positive view of volunteering in their community, even though only about two-thirds said they donate time, money or the like at least once per month. If Irie Foundation is to increase the amount of free programs offered to coincide with the opening of Irie Rhythms Academy, they are sure to need an increase in the amount of people volunteering to help facilitate and coordinate these programs. To do this, along with increasing its overall awareness, the Foundation will have to have a large outreach effort for volunteers, and once they acquire those volunteers, implement creative ways to develop a strong passion for the work the Foundation is doing.

First, Irie Foundation will need to get a sizable amount of volunteers, while also being sure to only recruit people who are really aiming to make a difference and who are passionate about the Foundation's mission. This will be a fine line to walk, as they want to most definitely increase their volunteer numbers, but do not want to allow just anyone to be so closely associated with their work, to ensure the Irie Foundation brand is meaningful and portrayed positively even outside of structured programs.

One method that could prove useful in recruiting volunteers is increasing outreach on social media. While Facebook would be the most useful for Generation X outreach, as 100 percent of the people interviewed said they were active on Facebook, reaching Millennials can be done by way of both Instagram and Facebook, as 100 percent of respondents were active on both platforms. Since 80 percent of Millennials and 75 percent of Generation Xers said they volunteer at least once per month, both groups would be ideal candidates to direct promotions for volunteering opportunities.

Next, the Foundation will have to ensure their volunteers are seeing the effects of the time and effort they are putting forth. This identification of making a positive impact will help volunteers realize just how much they contribute and will ultimately increase the likelihood of them remaining with the organization. Lastly, as people tend to feel a strong connection to the community in which they reside, part of that connection is the other people who also live in that community. The idea of helping others in the community who need it most can be associated with uplifting the entire community, which makes people more prideful about where they are living, as well as positive about the prospects and well-being of the community.

III. Children Specific

Of the people surveyed, about 68 percent had children who participate in after school programs ranging from sports, to performing arts, to tutoring or academically-focused courses. While children participating in these programs are sure to learn the inherent skills that come with these activities, such as kicking a soccer ball, playing the clarinet or scoring well on an exam, the parents surveyed said that what they like most about these programs are the "soft skills" their children are learning. Additionally, parents noted that they believe these programs are helping their children gain the necessary attributes needed to succeed in the workplace alongside other people.

For Irie Foundation, this means that regardless of the programs they are holding, they need to consider the skills that they want the participating children to walk away with that are secondary and come as a result of the work and effort put into learning that new skill or improving their knowledge. Since 100 percent of people interviewed said they acknowledge the value of arts in education and respondents whose children participate in different types of extracurricular programs had a desire for their kids to learn soft skills, Irie Foundation should highlight the skills that are geared toward communication and interaction that children will learn from their programs. Not only will this satisfy the parents of these children, who are putting an emphasis on acquiring soft skills, it will benefit the children when they move onto a career or another take on another hobby to which they can transfer these skills.

Even the people whose children were not involved in any performing arts related programming still acknowledged that incorporating arts is beneficial to a child's education. This shows that the arts are valued and supported, even among people whose first choice might not be to enroll their children into a performing arts program.

Expanding on this and putting an emphasis on the benefits of arts education, Irie Foundation will have a greater likelihood of drawing more students to participate in their programs ahead of the opening of Irie Rhythms Academy, a center geared toward educating using a STEAM curriculum. If Irie Foundation is looking to expand their scope and help even more children, it would be valuable to add more programs in areas like sports and physical activities for students whose preference is these activities.

Conclusion

After analyzing all of the research, the teams are prepared to draw several conclusions. The mission of Irie Foundation is one that many would be willing to support through volunteering time or donating money, skills or resources. Even though Irie Foundation has quite a ways to go as far as brand and mission recognition, the opening of Irie Rhythms Academy could serve as a fresh charge of spirit into the organization, complete with new programming and more opportunity to benefit at-risk youth.

Some steps that could be implemented to increase the chance of making the most of the opening of Irie Rhythms Academy is the creation of more programs that are teaching children tangible skills like performing arts, while also emphasizing the development of personal attributes that can be transferred to other areas in their lives. A new wave of volunteers who are passionate about working with children and bettering their community must be recruited to take part in managing and facilitating these programs if they are to be a success.

Even in a highly saturated philanthropic market like South Florida, Irie Foundation can use this information as a basis to set themselves apart from their competition and other nonprofits in the community, and put themselves in the best position of being successful in their mission of improving the lives of at-risk youth.

9

IRIE WEEKEND &
IRIE FOUNDATION
STYLE GUIDE

COLOR PALETTE

    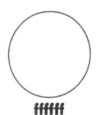 

086993   E53B54   23A6E0   ADA60A   ffffff   000000

TYPEFACES

FUTURA BOLD   GOTHAM BOOK REGULAR

INSPIRATION

Irie Foundation and Irie Weekend Writing Style Guide

Irie Foundation
Official Name:
Irie Foundation
> Second Reference: The Foundation
> Second Reference: If discussed in the middle of a sentence, Irie Foundation should be referred to as "the Foundation"

About Irie Foundation:
Irie Foundation is a year-round not for profit organization working to create positive impacts for South Florida's at-risk youth. The foundation seeks to inspire children from middle school onward to pursue higher education, assisting them on their journey toward becoming successful adults. The Foundation is supported by sponsors, partners and fundraising events.

Year Founded:
2011 by DJ Irie

Irie Foundation Address:
Irie Foundation
% Big Brothers and Big Sisters of Greater Miami
550 NW 42nd Ave., Fourth Floor
Miami, FL, 33126
United States of America

Phone Number:
(305) 497-2665

Email:
info@iriefoundation.org

Official Building Name:
Irie Rhythms Academy
4th Floor of the Carnival Center for Excellence

Irie Rhythms Academy Address:
Irie Rhythms Academy
% Big Brothers and Big Sisters of Greater Miami
550 NW 42nd Ave., Fourth Floor
Miami, FL, 33126
United States of America

About Irie Rhythms Academy:
Irie Foundation partnered with Carnival Foundation, Miami Heat Charitable Fund and Big Brothers Big Sisters of Miami to create a state-of-the-art education and technology center located on the fourth floor of the new Carnival Center for Excellence building. This center, known as the

Irie Foundation Special Events: Tactical Plan

Goal: Promotion

I. **Objective 1:** Increase engagement for Irie Rhythms Academy among corporate audiences, celebrities and the general public by 30 percent from the grand-opening day to end of December 2018.

    A. **Strategy**: Generate media coverage

        Tactic 1: Create a Media Kit for Irie Rhythms Academy's Mic Drop

            i. Advisory—Irie Rhythms Academy's Mic Drop (App. C. 1. d.)

            ii. Brochure—Irie Rhythms Academy building, programming and special programming events (App. E. 3. a.)

            iii. Fact Sheet—Irie Rhythms Academy building, programming and special programming events (App. E. 5. a.)

            iv. Feature Story—Irie Rhythms Academy's Mic Drop Recap (App. C. 2. f.)

            v. Invitations—Inviting celebrities to Irie Rhythms Academy's Mic Drop (App. E. 9. c.)

            vi. Media Lists—List for local and non-profit based media (App. B. 3. c. f.)

            vii. Pitch—Irie Rhythms Academy's Mic Drop (App. C. 3. c.)

            viii. Release—Irie Rhythms Academy's Mic Drop (App. C. 4. b.)

            ix. Release—Post- Irie Rhythms Academy's Mic Drop Recap (App. C. 4. e.)

            x. Social Media—Facebook, Instagram and Twitter posts specific to Irie Rhythms Academy's Mic Drop (App. D. 2)

            xi. Web—Announcing Irie Rhythms Academy's Mic Drop (App. C. 5. b.)

        Tactic 2: Create a Media Kit for Irie Foundation's All Day Art Extravaganza

            i. Advisory—Irie Foundation's All Day Art Extravaganza (App. C. 1. c.)

            ii. Evite—Inviting Irie Foundation parents to sign their child up for Irie Foundation's All Day Art Extravaganza (App. E. 4. b.)

            iii. Feature Story—Irie Foundation's All Day Art Extravaganza Concert (App. C. 2. b.)

            iv. Media Lists—Lists for art-based, local, nonprofit-based (App. B. 3. a. f. c.)

            v. Pitch—Irie Foundation's All Day Art Extravaganza (App. C. 3. b.)

            vi. Release—Irie Foundation's All Day Art Extravaganza (App. C. 4. c.)

            vii. Social Media—Facebook, Instagram and Twitter posts specific to Irie Foundation's All Day Art Extravaganza (App. D. 2)

            viii. Web—Announcing Irie Foundation's All Day Art Extravaganza (App. C. 5. a.)

Tactic 3: Create a Media Kit for Irie Foundation's Battle of the DJs
    i. Advisory—Irie Foundation's Battle of the DJs (App. C. 1. a.)
    ii. Evite—Inviting Irie Foundation participants and their parents to Irie Foundation's Battle of the DJs (App. E. 4. c.)
    iii. Feature Story—Irie Foundation's Battle of the DJs (App. C. 2. a.)
    iv. Invitations—Inviting celebrities to Irie Foundation's Battle of the DJs (App. E. 9. a.)
    v. Media Lists—Lists for local, nonprofit-based, national, music-based (App. B. 3. c. d. f.)
    vi. Pitch—Irie Foundation's Battle of the DJs (App. C. d.)
    vii. Release—Irie Foundation's Battle of the DJs (App. C. 4. a.)
    viii. Release—Post-Irie Foundation's Battle of the DJs (App. C. 4. f.)
    ix. Social Media—Facebook, Instagram and Twitter posts specific to Irie Foundation's Battle of the DJs (App. D. 2.)
    x. Web—Announcing Irie Foundation's Benefit Concert and Battle of the DJs voting (App. C. 5. d. f.)

Tactic 4: Create a Media Kit for Irie Foundation's Gobble 'Till You Wobble
    i. Evite—Wishing Irie Foundation parents a 'Happy Thanksgiving' and informing them of the event that their child can participate in (App. E. 4. e.)
    ii. Evite—Inviting Irie Foundation alumni to the event (App. E. 4. a.)
    iii. Evite—Alumni thank you following Irie Foundation's Gobble 'Till You Wobble (App. E. 4. d.)
    iv. Feature Story— Irie Foundation's Gobble 'Till You Wobble (App. C. 2. c.)
    v. Social Media— Facebook, Instagram and Twitter posts specific to Irie Foundation's Gobble 'Till You Wobble (App. D. 2.)
    vi. Web—Announcing Irie Foundation's Gobble 'Till You Wobble (App. C. 5. c.)

Tactic 5: Create a Media Kit for Irie Foundation's Benefit Concert
    i. Advisory—Irie Foundation's Benefit Concert (App. C. 1. b.)
    ii. Feature Story—Irie Foundation's Benefit Concert (App. C. 2. d.)
    iii. Invitations—Inviting celebrities and Irie Foundation parents to Irie Foundation's Benefit Concert (App. E. 9. b.)
    iv. Media Lists—Lists for local, nonprofit-based, national, music-based (App. B. 3. b. c. f.)
    v. Pitch—Irie Foundation's Benefit Concert (App. C. 3. a.)
    vi. Release—Irie Foundation's Benefit Concert (App. C. 4. d.)
    vii. Release—Post-Irie Foundation's Benefit Concert (App. C. 3. g.)

Irie Foundation Special Events: Tactical Outline

Name: All Day Art Extravaganza

Description: 'All Day Art Extravaganza' allows current Irie Foundation participants to actively create different forms of art throughout the day with the help of college student volunteers. Students spend the day learning about the visual arts (drawing, painting, watercolors, graphic design, photography and more). This fun event exposes the children to different art forms with the intended outcome being that they find one they enjoy. Furthermore, a whole day of art allows these underserved, at-risk youth to relax and forget about their struggles. The art produced at this event is showcased and auctioned off at the gala during Irie Weekend, where the biggest corporate sponsors of the Foundation are. Showcasing the children's art here creates awareness of the Foundation's efforts and helps bridge the gap between the Foundation and the Weekend. Additionally, Irie Foundation produces a book with approximately 23 art pieces created during the Foundation's All Day Art Extravaganza. This book is printed and available for donors to look at and purchase during the gala. A smaller version of the book is included as a memento for the attendees of the gala.

When: Monday, Feb. 19, 2018 (President's Day, Day off of School)
Begins at 8 a.m., lunch break at 12-1 p.m., ends at 7 p.m.

Where: Irie Rhythms Academy
℅ Big Brothers and Big Sisters of Greater Miami
550 NW 42nd Ave., Fourth Floor
Miami, FL, 33126
United States of America

Who: Current participants in Irie Foundation programming that qualify as underserved, at-risk youth in Miami-Dade County in public schools from middle school to high school. More specifically, Generation Z.

Volunteers at the Irie Foundation, mostly from Generation Y. More specifically, volunteers are college students that focus their academic efforts on the arts, whether it be graphic design, painting, drawing, photography or any other form of visual arts.

How: Preparation:
- Irie Foundation must propose the idea of the All Day Art Extravaganza to the children in their current programming and explain the details.
- Irie Foundation must distribute flyers to the students in order to take home to their parents so they're aware of the event.
- Irie Foundation must gather the supplies, if they don't have them already, which include: brushes, paint, paper, watercolor, etc.

- Irie Foundation, with volunteers, must create different stations that have different activities for the children—watercolor, drawing, painting, graphic designing, etc.
- Irie Foundation must finalize the different art stations and create a rotation for the students. The time spent at each station is dependent on how many stations are selected by the Foundation.
- Irie Foundation must finalize the list of children that are attending the event. From there, they separate the children in groups to ensure they're rotating through all the stations.

Art Experience:
- The children arrive at Irie Rhythms Academy at 8 a.m. on Monday, Feb. 19, 2018.
- There is a 30 minute window to wait for all the children to arrive before allowing them to start rotating through the stations.
- Children are placed into their groups upon arrival and wait in their groups until art creation begins at 8:30 a.m. From there, they go to their first station. The rotation through stations depends on how much time the children spend at each station and how many stations there are.
- Children have a small 15 minute break for snack time at 10:30 a.m. and then return to their art stations.
- Children are provided with lunch at 12 p.m. and then return to their art stations when done.
- Children have a small 15 minute break for snack time at 3:30 p.m. and then return to their art stations when done.
- Children are provided with dinner at 6 p.m. and then return to their art stations when done.
- Children begin clean-up time at around 6:30 p.m. and collect the art pieces they want to take home.
- Children are released to leave after 7 p.m.

Volunteers:
- Irie Foundation must recruit volunteers to participate in the All Day Art Extravaganza.
- Irie Foundation should consider inviting college students whose academics are focused on the arts, in order to teach the students properly. More specifically, college students would be able to teach the children graphic design in simpler terms.
- Irie Foundation provides the volunteers the list of groups and station rotations (including the length of each station).
- The volunteers help set-up the different art stations to ensure all the right supplies are in place before the children arrive. For example, volunteers ensure there are paint brushes, watercolor paints and paper at the watercolor painting station.

Budget:

Item	Company	Quantity	Cost
Water	Zephyrhills	5 24-packs	$19.95
Soft Drinks (Coca-Cola, Diet Coca-Cola, Sprite, Fanta)	Coca-Cola	4 24-packs (one of each)	$72.26
Snacks *(Up to Irie Foundation's discretion)*	TBD		TBD
Lunch for the children	Domino's Pizza	8 large pizzas	$79.92
Dinner for the children *(Up to Irie Foundation's discretion)*	TBD		TBD
Flyers to promote the Art Program to the children and their families	FedEx	100 one-sided flyers	$59.98
Matting Paper	Amazon.com	2 25-packs	$14.54
Frames *(prices might vary depending on the size of the art showcased in the gala)*	Amazon.com	A minimum of 5 Frames	
8.5 X 11 spiral bound booklet created with the 23 chosen pieces	MgxCopy	Enough for each person that attends the gala (around 200 copies)	$846.00
Drawing tickets	Walmart	500 tickets	$6.05

Irie Foundation Special Events: Tactical Outline

Name: Battle of the DJs

Description: 'Battle of the DJs' allows children currently involved in Irie Foundation the opportunity to showcase their talents and shine in a DJ competition that brings members of the community together as they vote for the Irie Foundation participant with the best DJ-themed performance on stage. Irie Foundation participants have the opportunity to rehearse, combining the skillsets they've learned at Irie Rhythms Academy with that of a guest celebrity mentor, and then show off their talents during a Foundation hosted event. A panel of judges at the event rates the performances and gives their critiques, however it is truly up to members of the community to get involved and vote. Every performance at the event must to be uploaded to Irie Foundation's website. From here, members of the community can visit the website and vote for their top five performances. This voting link is to be shared via. Irie Foundation's social media platforms. One month later, the top five winners are announced and DJ Irie picks the grand-prize winner who must recreate their performance live on stage at Irie Weekend.

When: Tuesday, May 1, 2018: Irie Foundation Participant Rehearsal Begins
Monday, May 14, 2018: Irie Foundation Celebrity Visit
Friday, June 1, 2018 at 8 p.m.: Irie Foundation Battle of the DJs Event
Saturday, June 2, 2018: Irie Foundation Battle of the DJs Contest Begins
Friday, June 29, 2018 at 12 p.m. (ET): Irie Foundation Battle of the DJs Contest Ends
Saturday, June 30, 2018: Irie Foundation Battle of the DJs Winner Announced

Where: Irie Rhythms Academy
℅ Big Brothers and Big Sisters of Greater Miami
550 NW 42nd Ave., Fourth Floor
Miami, FL 33126
United States of America

Who: Generation Z, current participants in Irie Foundation programming who qualify as underserved, at-risk youth in Miami-Dade County from middle school to high school.

Baby Boomers, members of Generation Y and members of Generation X that are looking to get more involved and give back to the community.

How: Irie Foundation Contest Rules:
- Current Irie Foundation participants, the children involved in Irie Foundation programming, are eligible to participate in this contest.
- All participants must create a 1-2 minute on stage performance centered around DJ'ing; whether that be actively DJ'ing on stage, dancing to DJ beats, singing to a mix-tape, etc.

- If participants exceed the 2-minute maximum, he/she/they must be eliminated.
- Students may partner up with other members of Irie Foundation for their act, however no more than three people are allowed per group.
- Students must get their act approved by Irie Foundation prior to participating in Battle of the DJs.
- Any inappropriate behavior both on stage and during rehearsal time results in automatic disqualification and that student(s) is/are sent home immediately.
- A panel of judges rate students' performances based on originality, creativity, skill, effort and their level of interaction with the crowd.
- Every performance must be uploaded to Irie Foundation's website with the judges' comments beneath it.
- Members of the community have one month to visit Irie Foundation's website and vote for their five favorite performances. All votes after Friday, June 29, 2018 at 12 p.m. (ET) are not counted.
- Once the five performances with the most votes are announced, DJ Irie must pick the grand-prize winner.
- It is completely up to DJ Irie's discretion whom the grand-prize winner is.

Irie Foundation Participant Rehearsal:
- Irie Foundation must present the idea of participating in a DJ competition to current members of the Foundation—noting that the top five winners are featured on Irie Foundation's website and social media, and that the grand-prize winner gets the opportunity to perform at Irie Weekend among other celebrities.
- Irie Foundation must read the contest rules to all students, assuring that Irie Foundation participants understand.
- All Irie Foundation students that want to participate in Battle of the DJs must get a parental signature prior to participating.
- Irie Foundation must build in rehearsal time into their regular curriculum, working with students to help them create a DJ-themed performance on stage showcasing their individual talents and preparing them for the live showcase.
- Irie Foundation must teach these children how to use the spin tables and create their own mixes, all the while supplying them with the necessary tools to do so.
- Irie Foundation must assist students with vocal lessons, dancing, etc. based on individuals' acts and the talent they choose to showcase during Battle of the DJs.

Irie Foundation Celebrity Visit:
- Irie Foundation must set up a day where a celebrity DJ or music artist comes in and helps Irie Foundation participants with their music and acts.

- The grand-prize winner is announced through a video of DJ Irie himself with the student. This video must be posted to Irie Foundation's social media platforms and its website.
- The grand-prize winner performs at Irie Weekend.

Budget:

Item	Company	Quantity	Cost
Water	Zephyrhills	5 24-packs	$19.95
Soft Drinks (Coca-Cola, Diet Coca-Cola, Sprite, Fanta)	Coca-Cola	4 24-packs (one of each)	$72.96
Print-At-Home Tickets	Irie Foundation	100	$0
Party Streamers	Crepe-Paper	5 rolls	$5.45
Balloons	Party City	12 12" Decorative Assortment Balloons	$12.95
Invitations	FedEx	200 Custom Invitations Printed, Mailed Out	$155.00
Evites	Adobe InDesign	200	$0
Poster	FedEx	2 22x28" posters	$139.98
Flyers	FedEx	100 one-sided flyers	$59.98

Irie Foundation Special Events: Evaluations and Measurements

In order to measure the campaign's success, it is essential for Irie Foundation to have a plan for evaluating whether the goal and objectives were accomplished.

*For the below measurements, **On-Key** equates to a job well-done that is excellently executed, **Flat** equates to a sufficient job that still needs work and **Off-Key** equates to a fail that must be improved and re-evaluated for the future.*

I. **Objective 1:** Increase engagement for Irie Rhythms Academy among corporate audiences, celebrities and the general public by 30 percent from the grand-opening day to end of December 2018.

    A. **Strategy**: Generate media coverage

    Measurement:

        -Increased amount of media coverage in target publications about Irie Foundation and/or Irie Rhythms Academy by 60% or more = **On-Key**

        -Increased amount of media coverage in target publications about Irie Foundation and/or Irie Rhythms Academy by 30-59% = **Flat**

        -Increased amount of media coverage in target publications about Irie Foundation and/or Irie Rhythms Academy by 29% or less = **Off-Key**

    Evaluation:

        -Monitor and track how much media coverage Irie Foundation and Irie Rhythms Academy garnered using media coverage trackers and compare the total number at the end of Dec. 2018 to that of the previous year.

        -Break down publications by tier; giving your tier 1 publications (the best publications) 3 points for successfully landing a story. Examples of tier 1 publications include:

            -Newspaper: *US Today*

            -Magazine: *Rolling Stones*

            -Television: *Access Hollywood*

    Give your tier 2 publications (your medium level publications) 2 points for successfully landing a story. Examples of tier 2 publications include:

            -Newspaper: *Miami Herald*

            -Magazine: *Ocean Drive*

            -Television: *Deco Drive*

    Give your tier 3 publications (your lowest level publications) 1 point for successfully landing a story. Examples of tier 3 publications include:

            -Blogs: *Black Tie South Florida*

            -Television: *Miami-Dade TV*

    Compare the total number of points at the end of Dec. 2018 to that of the previous year.

    B. **Strategy**: Consistently engage with target audience to remain top-of-mind

    Measurement:

        -Increased number of Irie Foundation and Irie Rhythms Academy likes, shares, comments, new friends and mentions on social media by the general public by 50% or more = **On-Key**

-Increased number of Irie Foundation and Irie Rhythms Academy likes, shares, comments, new friends and mentions on social media by the general public by by 30-49% = **Flat**

-Increased number of Irie Foundation and Irie Rhythms Academy likes, shares, comments, new friends and mentions on social media by the general public by 29% or less = **Off-Key**

Evaluation:

-Count the number of likes Irie Foundation receives on their social media posts and give them 1 point for every like. Compare the total number of points at the end of Dec. 2018 to that of the previous year.

-Count the number of shares Irie Foundation receives on their social media posts and give them 2 points for every share. Compare the total number of points at the end of Dec. 2018 to that of the previous year.

-Count the number of comments Irie Foundation receives on their social media posts and give them 2 points for every comment. Compare the total number of points at the end of Dec. 2018 to that of the previous year. Note who these comments were made by and differentiate how many of the comments were from Irie Foundation, DJ Irie and Irie Foundation staff, compared to members of the public.

-Count the number of new friends that add Irie Foundation on their social media platforms and give them 3 points for every new friend. Compare the total number of points at the end of Dec. 2018 to that of the previous year.

-Count the number of mentions about Irie Foundation on externally curated posts and give them 3 points for every mention. Compare the total number of points at the end of Dec. 2018 to that of the previous year.

II.   **Objective 2:** Increase awareness through specialty programming events that create traffic for Irie Rhythms Academy by 30 percent by the end of December 2018.

A. **Strategy**: Generate media coverage

Measurement:

-Increased amount of media coverage in target publications about Irie Foundation and/or Irie Rhythms Academy by 60% or more = **On-Key**

-Increased amount of media coverage in target publications about Irie Foundation and/or Irie Rhythms Academy by 30-59% = **Flat**

-Increased amount of media coverage in target publications about Irie Foundation and/or Irie Rhythms Academy by 29% or less = **Off-Key**

Evaluation:

-Monitor and track how much media coverage Irie Foundation and Irie Rhythms Academy garnered using media coverage trackers and compare the total number at the end of Dec. 2018 to that of the previous year.

-Break down publications by tier; giving your tier 1 publications (the best publications) 3 points for successfully landing a story. Examples of tier 1 publications include:

-Newspaper: *US Today*

-Magazine: *Rolling Stones*

-Television: *Access Hollywood*

Irie Foundation Special Events: Recommendations

Thank You's

In the future, Irie Foundation should send out digital "thank you's" after special events in order to continue to engage their audience and show their appreciation toward them. These "thank you's" are recommended to be sent through email, as it is the most cost effective. The target audience of these "thank you's" would vary per event, but could include donors, volunteers, alumni and parents of children. Irie Foundation could use the "thank you's" to promote their newsletter and social media to increase community engagement with The Foundation. This would satisfy the Objective 1 and Strategy B.

Fact Sheet With Pricing for Irie Rhythms Academy

In the future, Irie Foundation should create a fact sheet with the prices of renting out spaces at Irie Rhythms Academy once that is finalized. The client expressed its desire to use the renting of these facilities in order to fund Irie Rhythms Academy. Thus, a fact sheet that is available to the public will make them aware that the state-of-the-art utilities are accessible to them. Furthermore, it's recommended to send these to specific celebrities, recording labels and anyone involved in the music or photography industry. This would satisfy Objective 1 and Strategy A. It would also satisfy Objective 2 and Strategy A.

School Year Wrap-Up Booklets

It is recommended to create booklets of artwork and pictures the end of every school year to be handed out as keepsakes during Irie Weekend, more specifically the Gala. These books should be used alongside the book of artwork from the All Day Art Experience. The school year wrap up booklets will showcase what the children of The Foundation were working on throughout the entirety of the year. Thus, showcasing how Irie Foundation aids children in learning with the STEAM programming. The purpose is to convince people to support The Foundation more during Irie Weekend if they see the impact it's made on the lives of children. This recommendation would satisfy the Objective 5 and Strategy A.

Survey After Irie Weekend

Send out a survey at the end of Irie Weekend 2019, asking Irie Weekend participants to answer. One of the questions within this survey should ask "What do you believe is the purpose of Irie Weekend?" with one of the answers reading "to raise money for additional programming and resources for the underserved, at-risk youth Irie Foundation helps." Surveys can also be distributed during events at Irie Weekend. The amount of people that select this response should be compared to the total number of Irie Weekend attendees. This would test Objective 5 and Strategy A and how effective they were.

Appendix

A. TIMELINE

B. MEDIA PLAN
1. Tactical Media Calendar
2. Media Plan
3. Media List
   a. Art-Based Media List
   b. Event-Based Media List
   c. Local Media List
   d. Music-Based Media List
   e. National Media List
   f. Nonprofit-Based Media List
   g. Social Media Influencers

C. WRITING SAMPLES
1. Advisories
   a. Irie Foundation's Battle of the DJs Scratches Up the Stage
   b. Irie Foundation Hosts Inaugural Benefit Concert
   c. Irie Foundation's Ready to Get Crafty at the All Day Art Extravaganza
   d. Irie Rhythms Academy's Mic Drop and Official Grand-Opening is Here
2. Feature Stories
   a. Battle of the DJs Takes the Term "Competition" to the Next Level
   b. Drawing and Painting and Photography, Oh My!
   c. Irie Foundation Alumni #Inspires Foundation Participants at Gobble 'Till You Wobble
   d. Irie Foundation Student gets Recruited by Prestigious Dance Academy at Benefit Concert
   e. Irie Rhythms Academy Cuts the Cake
   f. Irie Rhythms Academy's Mic Drop Event Drops Jaws with its Food
3. Pitches
   a. Accompany Mr. 305 and Get a Behind-the-Scenes look at Irie Foundation's Benefit Concert
   b. Are you a well-rounded artist? Find out at Irie Foundation's All Day Art Experience
   c. Get an Exclusive First Look at Irie Foundation's New Irie Rhythms Academy
   d. Meet Nelly and Become an Irie Foundation Battle of the DJs Participant for the Day
4. Press Releases
   a. DJ Irie Declares Battle of the DJs Grand-Prize Winner
   b. DJ Irie, Usher and Pitbull Perform at Irie Rhythms Academy's Mic Drop
   c. Irie Foundation Channels its Inner Britto at the All Day Art Extravaganza

       d. Join 'Mr. 305' Himself for an Intimate Concert Supporting Underserved Youth
       e. Kick-Off 2018 with DJ Irie at Irie Rhythms Academy's Mic Drop
       f. Nelly Makes Irie Foundation's Battle of the DJs a Smash Hit
       g. Pitbull Helps Raise $100,000 for Irie Foundation
   5. Web Blurbs
       a. Channel Your Inner Britto at Irie Foundation's All Day Art Extravaganza
       b. Irie Foundation Invites You to Irie Rhythms Academy's Mic Drop
       c. Irie Foundation Launches Gobble 'Till You Wobble
       d. Irie Foundation Presents Battle of the DJs, the Biggest DJ Competition of the Year
       e. See Pitbull Perform Live at Irie Foundation's Benefit Concert
       f. Vote for Your Favorite Battle of the DJs Star

D. SOCIAL MEDIA STRATEGY
   1. Social Media Audit
   2. Social Media Calendar

E. DESIGN SAMPLES
   1. Backgrounder
       a. Informing about Irie Rhythms Academy building, programming and special programming events
   2. Banner Advertisements
       a. Announcing Irie Foundation's All Day Art Experience
       b. Announcing Irie Foundation's Battle of the DJs
       c. Announcing Irie Foundation's Benefit Concert
       d. Announcing Irie Foundation's Gobble 'Till You Wobble
       e. Announcing Irie Rhythms Academy Mic Drop
       f. Battle of the DJs Voting Has Closed
       g. Battle of the DJs We Need Your Vote
   3. Brochure
       a. Informing about Irie Rhythms Academy building, programming and special programming events
   4. Evites
       a. Inviting alumni to Irie Foundation's Gobble 'Till You Wobble
       b. Inviting celebrities and Irie Foundation parents to Irie Foundation's All Day Art Experience
       c. Inviting people to participate in Battle of the DJs
       d. Thanking Irie Foundation Alumni
       e. Wishing Irie Foundation parents a 'Happy Thanksgiving'
       f. Wishing Irie Foundation parents 'Happy Holidays'
   5. Fact Sheet
       a. Informing about Irie Rhythms Academy building, programming and special programming events
   6. Flyers
       a. Announcing Irie Foundation's All Day Art Experience
       b. Announcing Irie Foundation's Battle of the DJs

           c. Announcing Irie Foundation's Benefit Concert
           d. Announcing Irie Foundation's Gobble 'Till You Wobble
           e. Announcing Irie Rhythms Academy Mic Drop
    7. Merchandise
           a. Irie Foundation Dad Hats
           b. Irie Foundation Drawstring Bags
           c. Irie Foundation Pencil Cases
    8. Newsletter
           a. Highlighting Irie Foundation participants at Irie Rhythms
              Academy
    9. Paper Invitations
           a. Inviting celebrities and Irie Foundation parents to Irie
              Foundation's Battle of the DJs
           b. Inviting celebrities and Irie Foundation parents to Irie
              Foundation's Benefit Concert
           c. Inviting celebrities and Irie Foundation parents to Irie Rhythms
              Academy Mic Drop
   10. Posters
           a. Promoting Irie Foundation's Battle of the DJs
           b. Promoting Irie Foundation's Benefit Concert
           c. Promoting Irie Rhythms Academy Mic Drop

F. PRIMARY RESEARCH
    1. Interview Questions
    2. Interview Results

G. SECONDARY RESEARCH
    1. Reference List
    2. Original Articles

H. POWERPOINT FOR THE CLIENT

Irie Foundation Special Events: Media Plan

This media plan outlines when Irie Foundation should distribute tactical writing pieces to varying media outlets. The various items inform the press of events coming up, activities occurring at Irie Rhythms Academy and other important Irie Foundation news. The media plan consists of several items including media advisories, media alerts, press releases, pitches, feature stories, web blurbs, a backgrounder and a fact sheet. Additionally, the media plan includes media lists that distinguish who these tactical writing pieces must be sent to.

Tactical Writing Pieces
Irie Rhythms Academy's Mic Drop
Media Advisory: Irie Rhythms Academy's Mic Drop and Official Grand-Opening is Here –
This media advisory is a brief announcement to the media discussing Irie Rhythms Academy's grand-opening event. It provides members of the media basic information regarding what the event is, when it is, where it is, who specifically the event is targeting and where to obtain tickets. This media advisory makes sure journalists know far in advance about Irie Rhythms Academy's Mic Drop, so they can mark it on their calendar, plan around the date and cover it.

Press Release: Kick-Off 2018 with DJ Irie at Irie Rhythms Academy's Mic Drop –
This press release serves as a detailed announcement for members of the media, containing both basic information about Irie Rhythms Academy's Mic Drop and additional information such as special quotes or details that highlight the event in a standout way. For this press release, Kyle Post, Director of Irie Foundation, is quoted discussing Irie Rhythms Academy's Mic Drop and the importance behind it.

Press Release: DJ Irie, Usher and Pitbull Perform at Irie Rhythms Academy's Mic Drop –
This press release serves as a follow-up release after Irie Rhythms Academy's Mic Drop event. It assures that the event, as well as Irie Foundation, remains top-of-mind even after the event occurs. It also includes important, newsworthy information and details that occurred throughout the night. Irie Foundation's Founder and CEO, DJ Irie, is quoted and highlighted, bringing in another newsworthy element for journalists to write about in their respective media outlets.

Pitch: Get an Exclusive First Look at Irie Foundation's New Irie Rhythms Academy –
This pitch gives specific media attention to a select journalist, inviting them for a private tour of Irie Rhythms Academy as well as the chance to serve as the emcee during the Mic Drop event. The pitch is a short letter to select media, offering them a special incentive to cover the event. This pitch is used to propel coverage from a simple calendar story to a focused feature story written about Irie Rhythms Academy's Mic Drop by the select journalist in attendance.

Feature Story: Irie Rhythms Academy's Mic Drop Event Drops Jaws with its Food –
This feature story was created with the intent to not be hard news, but instead something that is memorable and provides a human-interest aspect. This specific story highlights the local Miami restaurants that participated in Irie Rhythms Academy's Mic Drop event, and was written in a personable tone for readers to relate to. All feature stories were written to be included in Irie Foundation's newsletter: Transforming Tomorrow, that is to be sent out the first Monday of every month.

Feature Story: Irie Rhythms Academy Cuts the Cake –
This feature story was created with the intent to not be hard news, but instead something that is memorable and provides a human-interest aspect. This specific story highlights DJ Khaled surprising DJ Irie at the event with a cake commemorating the inaugural Mic Drop event. It was written in a light-hearted, personable tone for readers to relate to. All feature stories were written to be included in Irie Foundation's newsletter: Transforming Tomorrow, that is to be sent out the first Monday of every month.

Web Blurb: Irie Foundation Invites You to Irie Rhythms Academy's Mic Drop
This web blurb announces Irie Rhythms Academy's Mic Drop event on Irie Foundation's website so members of the community, as well as anyone else visiting the website, can stay up to date on all things happening at Irie Rhythms Academy.

Irie Foundation's All Day Art Extravaganza
Media Advisory: Irie Foundation's Ready to Get Crafty at the All Day Art Extravaganza –
This media advisory is a brief announcement to the media discussing Irie Foundation's All Day Art Extravaganza. It provides members of the media basic information regarding what the event is, when it is, where it is and who specifically the event is targeting. This media advisory makes sure journalists know far in advance about Irie Foundation's All Day Art Extravaganza, so they can mark it on their calendar, plan around the date and cover it.

Press Release: Irie Foundation Channels its Inner Britto at the All Day Art Extravaganza –
This press release serves as a follow-up release after Irie Foundation's All Day Art Extravaganza. It highlights Irie Foundation participants' interactions with University of Miami student volunteers, as well as all the art-filled rotations they experienced throughout the day. It also includes a quote from a University of Miami student volunteer, bringing in personal, different perspective on the event for journalists to write about in their respective media outlets.

Pitch: Are You a Well-Rounded Artist? Find Out at Irie Foundation's All Day Art Extravaganza –
This pitch gives specific media attention to a select journalist, inviting them to actively participate in Irie Foundation's All Day Art Extravaganza and interview the Irie Foundation participants as well as student volunteers. The pitch is a short letter to select media, offering them a special incentive to cover the event. This pitch is used to propel coverage from a simple calendar story to a focused feature story written about Irie Foundation's All Day Art Extravaganza by the select journalist in attendance.

Media Advisory
FOR IMMEDIATE RELEASE
Jan. 29, 2018

IRIE FOUNDATION'S READY TO GET CRAFTY AT THE ALL DAY ART EXTRAVAGANZA

What: Irie Foundation's All Day Art Extravaganza is an event that exposes underserved at-risk-youth in Miami-Dade to the arts with the goal of increasing their passion and knowledge of the field. Irie Foundation participants are taught about the visual arts including but not limited to: drawing, painting, watercolors, graphic design and photography with the help of college-aged volunteers studying or majoring in the arts. Furthermore, this day of art allows Irie Foundation participants to relax and forget about their struggles as they create masterpieces displayed at Irie Weekend 2018.

When: President's Day, Monday Feb. 19, 2018 — Irie Foundation's All Day Art Extravaganza begins at 8 a.m. with the commencement of art creation. There is a lunch break from 12-1 p.m. The event ends at 7 p.m. with the final collection of the art at 6:30 p.m. and a 30-minute clean-up segment.

Where: Irie Foundation
% Big Brothers and Big Sisters of Greater Miami
550 NW 42nd Ave., Fourth Floor
Miami, FL, 33126
United States of America

Who: Current participants in Irie Foundation programming that qualify as underserved, at-risk youth in Miami-Dade County public schools from middle school to High School.

Current volunteers at Irie Foundation and college-aged students within Miami-Dade County whose academic efforts are focused on the arts.

Irie Foundation seeks to empower South Florida's at-risk youth to lead productive lives through cultural experiences, mentorship programs and scholarship opportunities. By following the young people it serves from middle school through high school, the Foundation's focus is to inspire and encourage its students to graduate high school, pursue higher education in order to reach their goals and aspirations.

###

BATTLE OF THE DJS TAKES THE TERM "COMPETITION" TO THE NEXT LEVEL

On June 1, 2018, Irie Foundation held a competition, but not just your average rivalry where people watch as one person beats out another person at something. This competition was special. Why you may ask? Because it united underserved youth and at-risk children with members of the community, famous celebrities and noteworthy media, all under one roof for the common cause of DJ'ing.

Irie Foundation participants had been practicing since May 1, 2018, assuring that their DJ-themed performances were perfected for the big day. These performances ranged from actively DJ'ing on stage, dancing to DJ beats, singing to mix-tapes, breakdancing to different tunes and more. Every Irie Foundation participant utilized their own skills, along with those taught at Irie Rhythms Academy, to create a performance that allowed them to shine with confidence on stage.

Leading up to the event, world-renowned singer, songwriter and entrepreneur, Nelly, even came to Irie Foundation to help students with these performances. Nelly reiterated the importance of having fun with the DJ competition and not letting the concept of winning detract from the overall experience. With Nelly's visit, Irie Foundation participants became even more excited, working with him to learn special tricks that they could incorporate into their skillsets.

When the big day finally approached, students sat behind the curtains feeling an array of emotions: nervousness, excitement, fear, exhilaration. Every Irie Foundation participant had worked so hard for the past month, and all that hard work was finally being put to the test. As students peered out at the crowd from behind the curtains, their eyes immediately sparkled. To their surprise, the room was completely filled. Every seat in the audience was taken and those that couldn't find seats migrated to the standing areas. Family, friends, members of the community, everyone had come out to watch these Irie Foundation participants perform their hearts out; and it was this amount of support that really set the stage and the tone for the night.

After every child's performance, the crowd went wild. Applause, cheering, hollering, the community was beyond themselves. The panel of celebrity judges that rated each child's performance had nothing but positive things to say about each performance, building upon the confidence of Irie Foundation participants and growing their self-esteem.

Ultimately, it was the unified audience, full of diverse people from every demographic and psychographic, coming together for the common cause of the kids that sparked the night and made it one to never forget. What was this competition? Battle of the DJs, and it proved to be an undeniable success.

FOUNDATION

To: Cata Balzano
From: Felicia Quaning
Date: Feb. 1, 2018
Subject: Are you a well-rounded artist? Find out at Irie Foundation's All Day Art Experience

Dear Ms. Balzano,

This is Felicia from Irie Foundation, the only 501 (c)(3) not-for-profit organization offering underserved, at-risk youth in Miami-Dade County full access to state-of-the-art music and technology resources.

I read your article about Irie Weekend raising $90,000 for Irie Foundation and you truly highlighted the purpose of the Foundation and the #InspIRIE Kids Golf Clinic. It's clear you understand Irie Foundation's mission and values, making you the obvious choice for who we'd like to invite to our inaugural All Day Art Extravaganza.

We want you to join in on the fun as you create art with the underserved, at-risk youth we serve, putting yourself in their shoes for the day and experiencing Irie Foundation's All Day Art Extravaganza, followed by the opportunity to hand select your favorite art pieces to be shown at Irie Weekend 2018.

On Feb. 19, 2018, we ask that you arrive at Irie Rhythms Academy (550 NW 42nd Ave., Fourth Floor) at 8 a.m.; the same time Irie Foundation participants are arriving to gain the full Irie experience from start to finish. Throughout the day, we invite you to let loose and immerse yourself in creating art with several children and Irie Foundation volunteers, as you embark on art-filled rotations, learning about graphic design, photography, watercolor painting and more. As you switch between the art stations, you get the opportunity to talk with several children and volunteers to learn about the experiences they've had with Irie Foundation.

At the end of the day, you get to help Irie Foundation staff hand-select art pieces to showcase during Irie Weekend's 2018 Gala, as well as choose different art pieces for the All Day Art Experience print booklet. Kyle Post, Director of Irie Foundation, is then set to sit down with you and talk about Irie Foundation programming, discuss the kids Irie Foundation works to support and answer questions.

Expect my call Thursday to discuss the details and answer any additional questions you may have. In the meantime, feel free to reach out to me via email or phone.

Sincerely,
Felicia Quaning

Press Release
FOR IMMEDIATE RELEASE
June 30, 2018

DJ IRIE DECLARES BATTLE OF THE DJS GRAND-PRIZE WINNER
Irie Foundation's Battle of the DJs Grand-Prize Winner is Selected and Set to Perform at Irie Weekend 2018.

MIAMI — Irie Foundation announced the official grand-prize winner of Battle of the DJs, Susie Golightly. The 16-year-old DJ and vocalist wowed the judges, members of the community and DJ Irie himself with her turntable skills as she rocked the stage with her own beats.

Following Battle of the DJs, members of the community flooded Irie Foundation's website, voting for their top five favorite performances online after the live event. The top five winners as voted upon by the community were Susie with her live turntable performance, Jennifer with her singing performance, Steve with his breakdancing skills, Johnny with his breakdancing performance and Rebecca who dropped the beat. Every Irie Foundation performance was incredible, but these five winners sealed the deal their charisma on stage and uniqueness. Members of the community took to sharing these performances on their own social media platforms, encouraging their friends to vote as well, and ultimately Battle of the DJs became a viral sensation.

"All five Irie Foundation participants are top winners in my book, along with everyone else who participated," claims Founder and CEO of Irie Foundation, DJ Irie. "However, there can only be one grand-prize winner and Susie Golightly's positive energy, excitement and skills shined in her exceptional performance that I'm thrilled to see recreated at Irie Weekend 2018."

Susie Golightly is set to perform at Irie Weekend, Irie Foundation's signature annual benefit extravaganza that raises money for the Foundation's mission to positively impact the lives of South Florida's at-risk youth. After participating in Battle of the DJs on Friday, June 29, 2018, Golightly has been continually practicing her act with the hope of performing again live on-stage in front of thousands of people. For this lucky Irie Foundation participant, her dreams were granted and she can be seen on the main stage at Irie Weekend on July 1, 2018 at 6 p.m., opening up for no other than Cornell Haynes Jr. (aka Nelly).

Battle of the DJs had a packed house, with every seat in Irie Rhythms Academy filled with a guest anxiously awaiting Irie Foundation's DJ-themed performance. The kids did not disappoint, as 20 different Irie Foundation participants got up the courage to perform a live 1-2 minute

-more-performance on stage in front of the crowded room. A celebrity panel of judges consisting of DJ Irie, Nelly, Kevin Hart, and Clifford Harris Jr. (aka T.I.) rated each performance based on originality, creativity, skill, effort and crowd interaction. Golightly had earned one of the top ratings from the judges with a nearly perfect score, and these positive marks were re-emphasized as the community and DJ Irie also voted for her performance as a definitive standout.

To see Golightly's performance from Battle of the DJs and all of the other top winners' DJ-themed acts, visit Irie Foundation's website.

Irie Foundation seeks to empower South Florida's at-risk youth to lead productive lives through cultural experiences, mentorship programs and scholarship opportunities. By following the young people it serves from middle school through high school, the Foundation's focus is to inspire and encourage its students to graduate high school, pursue higher education in order to reach their goals and aspirations.

For More Information:

SPECIAL EVENTS

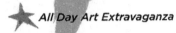
All Day Art Extravaganza

Children participate in creating different forms of art throughout the entire day. Students learn about the visual arts with the intended outcome that they find one they enjoy.

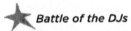
Battle of the DJs

Allows children currently involved in Irie Foundation the opportunity to showcase their talents and shine in a DJ competition that brings members of the Miami-Dade community together.

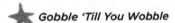
Gobble 'Till You Wobble

Thanksgiving themed event that brings alumni together with current Foundation participants for a day of games, activities and speakers.

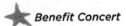
Benefit Concert

Special and intimate concert at Irie Rhythms Academy to bring the Miami-Dade Community together with children from the Foundation.

Mic Drop

Grand opening celebration of Irie Foundation's new state-of the-art education center for members of the Miami-Dade Community.

PROGRAMS

Cultural Passport Program

Provides engaging sociocultural experiences in the classroom and at off-campus field trips.

Impact Scholarship Fund

Scholarship fund, in partnership with Big Brothers Big Sisters that honors students with awards for their journey toward higher education.

Irie's Day of Service

A monthly volunteer event that provides students experience with serving their local community.

My Life Mentoring Presented by Jimmy John's

Mentoring meetings and quarterly report card conferences that help improve the academic success of at-risk youth.

Reach for the Stars

An annual event that welcomes celebrities to share their stories of success with our current students.

Shine Bright Semiannual Talent Showcase

An annual event that showcases the skills learned by students in the areas of musical performance

Student-to-Student

Connects college students with students to tutor them in school subjects with the goal of improving academic performance.

Suit-Up and Study-Up

A program held for 11th and 12th grade students that includes skill-building workshops and standardized test preparation courses to aid in graduation.

Superstar Summer Camp

A summer camp that uses STEAM curriculum to provide students a place to continue learning new skills during the summer months.

IRIE RHYTHMS ACADEMY

Irie Rhythms Academy is a state-of-the-art education and technology center located on the fourth floor of the Carnival Center for Excellence Building. Using a STEAM curricula and structured programming, Irie Foundation and its partners aim to improve academic performance and decrease after school violence for underserved youth.

Battle of the DJs

what :

Come out to see Irie
Foundation participants
show off their DJ skills, as
they're ranked by a celebrity
panel of judges. Prepare
for dancing, singing and a
mystery guest performance!

where :

Irie Rhythms Academy
550 NW 42nd Ave., Fourth Floor
Miami, FL 33126
United States of America

when :

Friday, June 1, 2018
at 8 p.m.

Tickets :

Sold on Irie Foundation's
website for $25

Drawing and Painting and Photography, Oh My

*W*atercolor paints spilled across the table on one side of the room, while marker-stained hands consistently reached for more paper on the other. In the room around the corner, a group of Irie Foundation participants sat with headphones on as they artfully crafted graphic design masterpieces using Adobe Photoshop. Another group of students walked around outside skillfully taking photographs of the scenery, while the last group of students did ceramics. All these chaotic and exciting art projects were happening simultaneously at Irie Foundation, as students participated in the Foundation's All Day Art Extravaganza.

Irie Foundation's All Day Art Extravaganza began bright and early on Monday, Feb. 19, 2018. Students arrived at Irie Rhythms Academy at 8 a.m., enthusiastic about the art they were going to make and anxious to get to work. Immediately upon arrival, each child was told that they were going to get very messy throughout the day; a concept these kids giggled at as they cheered with excitement. They rolled up their sleeves, split into groups and got straight to work,

diving into the multitude of art stations Irie Foundation set up for them. Students from the University of Miami volunteered to help the Foundation during the event, manning the different art stations and leading projects.

"I knew nothing about graphic design before Anastasia taught me how to use Photoshop during the All Day Art Extravaganza," said 15-year-old Marcos, an Irie Foundation participant. "By the end of the day, I felt like a pro. "

"When I grow up, I want a job in graphic design."

Many Irie Foundation participants felt similarly to Marcos, finding

different art projects that resonated with them and helped them discover a new underlying passion. Irie Foundation's All Day Art Extravaganza allowed children to work with different mediums and discover the calming sensation of creating art. While channeling their inner Brittos, many Irie Foundation participants found specific projects that they enjoyed and ultimately, that they'd want to continue practicing in their free time.

The artwork produced from Irie Foundation's All Day Art Extravaganza is extraordinary and standout pieces are to be entered into a drawing for Irie Weekend 2018. Attendees of the Weekend have the opportunity to purchase tickets and win different art pieces during the gala. Don't miss the opportunity to bring home a masterpiece!

GLOSSARY OF TERMS

Advertising: Paid media placements aimed to sell productions to targeted audiences.

Audience: The specific group of people who are identified as the target group or groups.

Budget: Monetary breakdown of the cost that pieces of the PR campaign are expected to cost the client.

Calendar/Timeline (Campaign): This is a comprehensive calendar that includes all tactical elements and outlines times for printing, delivery, dissemination and must include all press, design and event materials.

Ethics: Ethics are defined as the moral base that governs a person's behaviors and/or the ways in which a person makes decisions and takes action.

Evaluation: Determining the success or failure of objectives with a PR campaign or the whole project includes ongoing, summative and formative evaluation.

Goal: A goal statement is the broader and overarching results of the efforts. A goal statement, when written properly, is the opposing *mirror* of the issue statement. It should address the issues on a broad scale. Goal statements are not quantifiable, whereas objectives are defined and measureable.

Historic Figures: The founding figures of PR that include Edward Bernays, Ivy Lee and Betsy Plank.

Hype: The term *hype* is derived from *hyperbole*, which is an exaggeration to impress and evoke a strong response. No legitimate PR campaign achieves successful goals and hits the marks with the objectives using spin or hype.

Issue Statement: Issue statements are usually one sentence and are a summation of the overarching problem faced by the company and/or client that the campaign centers on resolving.

Marketing: Product promotions and placements aimed at specific audiences with the intent of leading to sales and activation. All marketing is based on products or services and although it may include messaging or behavioral shifts, the end objective is always tied to profits.

Media: Mainstream media consists of newspapers, magazines, television, radio and so on. Digital media consists of websites and social media.

Measurements: The *scale* by which a tactical element or elements within a campaign are graded to determine success, mediocrity or failure.

Objectives: Objectives are usually defined by time or focus. Depending on the overall timeframe of the campaign, objectives can be either short term or long term.

Primary Research: Research created by the PR professionals or an independent research group specific for the client or project. This is original work that is either qualitative or quantitative and requires analysis of the acquired data.

Public Relations: Public relations is a strategic communication process that builds mutually beneficial relationships between organizations and their publics. (PRSA)

Public Relations Campaigns: Modern PR campaigns present solutions to one goal. Broken down into measurable objectives, the tactics used to create successful campaigns are skills practitioners constantly fine-tune.

Public Relations Campaigns Types: The most common categories for persuasive PR campaigns are commercial, educational, political, reputation and social change.

Qualitative Research: Primary research that examines attitudes, perceptions and opinions. Tools to gather qualitative research include focus groups, interviews, observations and so on.

Quantitative Research: Primary research that examines behavioral choices through numerical data. Tools to gather quantitative research include surveys, questionnaires and polls.

Recommendations: Anything that can benefit a campaign that are unable to be included because of reasons beyond the scope of the project.

Secondary Research: This is the collection of previously completed research studies that have conclusions or results that are related to topics within the PR campaign. Secondary research summaries begin with an introduction to the topics, summaries by topic and conclusions.

Spin: The term *spin* usually refers to efforts to tilt the public perception in ways favorable to a political candidate or product. Unfortunately, it has a negative connotation and is often synonymous with the practice of PR. When used spin usually means the twisting of the truth to only highlight the positive and *dizzy* the audience.

Strategy: Connections made between the theory and tactical application that integrates bigger concepts with a method to accomplish the objectives.

Tactics: The created materials that are designed, written and planned as the outward facing pieces of a PR campaign that include the messaging and themes aimed to connect with a specific target audience.

Teamwork: The word *teamwork* usually evokes fear, panic and frustration. The reality however, is that in the modern workforce, teamwork is collective thinking models and shared workloads is more common than ever before.

INDEX